SPIRIT OF SUCCESS

THE SPROULE STORY

PENELOPE E. GREY AND LAURA J. KROWCHUK

SPROULE ASSOCIATES LIMITED

Canadian Cataloguing in Publication Data

Grey, Penelope E. (Penelope Elizabeth), 1955-
    Spirit of success

    Includes index.
    ISBN 0-9682550-0-0

    1.Sproule,John Campbell,1905-1970. 2.Sproule Associates--History.
3.Petroleum industry and trade—Alberta— History. 4.Petroleum industry and trade—Arctic regions— History. 5.Petroleum engineers—Alberta—Biography.
I. Krowchuk, Laura J.(Laura Jean),1961- II.Sproule Associates. III.Title.
HD9574.C22G74 1997   338.7'092   C97-910811-X

Research by Laura J. Krowchuk and Emily D. (Babs) MacInnes
Edited by Penelope (Penny) E. Grey
Typesetting and design by J.A. (Sandy) Irvine, By Design Services
Proofreading by Frances Purslow
Printed and bound in Canada by Friesens, Altona, MB

Sproule Associates Limited
900 140 Fourth Ave SW
Calgary AB Canada T2P 3N3
Telephone (403) 294-5500

DEDICATED TO THE MEMORY OF CAM SPROULE

TABLE OF CONTENTS

Acknowledgements

The authors would like to thank all those who contributed to the successful completion of this book: AAPG, AINA Library (Calgary), APEGGA (Edmonton), Hal Acheson, Duff Ackerley, Grey Alexander, Bill Anderson, John Andrichuk, Ian Armitage, Bob Armstrong, Jack Armstrong, Jan Bakhoven, Ed Baltrusaitis, Mary Barr, Gordon Barritt, Dora Bayerle, Norm Becker, Peter Bediz, Elmer Berlie, Bev Bernard, Diana Berry, Hal Bickel, Chuck Bily, Margaret and Bill Bowes, Jim Brown, Jack Browning, Dick Bruer, Mike Brusset, Alan Bryant, Charlie Bulmer, John Burns, Peter Burns, Canadian Association of Petroleum Producers (Calgary), CIM (Montreal), CSPG (Calgary), Calgary Public Library, Bryce Cameron, Don Campbell, Douglas Carsted, Ruby Leon Carter, Rudy Cech, John Chipperfield, Debbie Christie, City of Calgary Archives, Sandy Clancy, Noel Cleland, Don Cooke, Franky Cooper, Bud Coote, Eric Connelly, Steve Cosburn, Ken Crowther, *Daily Oil Bulletin* (Calgary), C.E. Davey, George DeMille, Department of Indian and Northern Affairs (Ottawa), Rein de Wit, David Dineley, Art Dixon, Wally Drew, Ken Drummond, Denny Duff, Charlie Dunkley, Jim Durkie, Tony Edgington, Aubrey Edwards, Bert Ellison, AEUB, Oscar Erdman, Lorne Fitch, Hans Firla, Neil Fluker, Yves Fortier, Glenn Fox, George Fukushima, Bill Furnival, George Furnival, Geological Association of Canada (Newfoundland), Geological Survey of Canada, Jack Gallagher, Hans Garde-Hansen, Dallas Hawkins, Ned Gilbert, Glenbow Museum (Calgary), Jean Gorrell, Grande Prairie Museum (Alberta), Grande Prairie Public Library, Jean Greig, Mickey Gulless, Bill Gussow, Haileybury School of Mines (Ontario), Ruby Haines, Bill Hancock, Lois and Stan Harding, Renny Haylock, Bob Heileg, Alex Hemstock, Warren Henker, Marmie Hess, Charles Hetherington, Dick Hill, Chuck Horne, Digby Hunt, George Hunter, John Hunter, ISPG Library (Calgary), Imperial Oil Archives (Toronto), Jim Ince, Sandy Irvine, Journal of Canadian Petroleum Technology

(Calgary), Gordon Jaremko, Inga Jensen, Gordon Jones, Stan Kanik, Hari Kapil, Morris Kilik, Peter Kreutzer, Walter Kupsch, Patrick Landes, Cindy Lavigne, Bora Lazic, Jean and Jack Leslie, Luke Lindoe, Vi Link, Ted Link Jr., Griff Lloyd, Punch Logan, Diane Loranger, James MacDonald, Emily (Babs) MacInnes, Keith MacLeod, Bob Manson, Marilyn Marsden, Blake Marshall, Bruce Marshall, Bob Matheson, Ulrich Mayr, Doreen McArthur, Marion and Gordon McCracken, Don McEachern, Anne McKenzie, Don McKinnon, Gordon McMillan, Andrew Miall, Earl Miller, Donna Misurelli, Susan Mundl-Cowper, Ruby and Roy Murray, National Archives of Canada (Ottawa), NEB, Jim Nemrava, Chuck Newmarch, Dr. John Noakes, Ken North, John Nugent, Jean O'Brien, Bob O'Connor, *Oilweek* magazine (Calgary), Panarctic Oils Ltd., Karen Patz, Stan Pearson, Nate Peterson, Petroleum Industry Oral History Project (Calgary), Coye Pfleger, Mike Plested, Polar Continental Shelf Project, Jack Porter, John Porter, Bob Pow, Jim Powell, Harold Rainforth, Leola (Hobbs) Reeve, Colin Risk, J.M. Robertson, Glenn Robinson, Hank Roessingh, Fred Roots, Royal Society of Canada (Ottawa), Alan Rudkin, Bill Sanderson, Wayne Sargent, William Sarjeant, Saskatchewan Energy and Mines, Henry Sawatzky, Gray and Gert Sharp, Clark Siferd, Zoltan Simon, Ken Sinclair, Lionel Singleton, Gordon Skilling, Clark Smith, Hubert Somerville, Southam Information (Calgary), Herb Spear, Judy Sproule, R.M. Stainforth, Charles Stelck, Nora Stewart, John Stuart Smith, Jean Suitor, Park Sullivan, Gordon Tapp, Don Taylor, Jim Terrill, Nora Tettensor, Brian Thomas, Roger Thomsen, Ray Thorsteinsson, Ed Tovell, Dorothea (Knudtson) Trouth, University of Alberta Archives (Edmonton), Gus Van Wielingen, John Wall, Max Ward, Bruce Watson, Henri Wennekers, Bob Wickenden, Dean M. Williams, Keith Williams, George Wilson, Bob Workum, Frank Wormsbecker, Anne Wright, Coote Wright-Broughton, Zoltan Zalan, and Anne Zoumer. Our sincere apologies if any contributor has been overlooked.

FOREWORD

When I ask myself why it is important to tell the Sproule story, I think about the man who founded a company I've been proud to be a part of for almost 25 years. I didn't have the privilege of meeting "Doc" Sproule, but I admire him greatly nevertheless. He had the vision to see the potential of Canadian oil and gas resources when only a few discoveries had been made, and he started a company that blended science and industry in a way that would take that company into the next century. Without him, Arctic exploration may never have got off the ground, and it seems sure that Panarctic Oils would never have happened. There is no doubt he was an outstanding geologist, a great leader, and a true Canadian. The answer to my question, then, is this: the story simply *had* to be told, before those who know the story best are gone.

The daunting task of telling the Sproule story fell to a large number of people, who allowed us to probe their memories of Cam Sproule and the people who worked with him. Writers Penny Grey and Laura Krowchuk did an excellent job of weaving a story out of those memories and from countless letters, published papers, and written contributions.

The authors have kindly recognized in their acknowledgements everyone who played a part in the successful completion of this project. I would like to personally thank Dr. Sproule's daughters, Anne and Judy, who made available all of their father's papers and who helped bring their father to life for us. The book would certainly not have been complete without them. Stan Harding, such an important individual in the history of Sproule, contributed greatly in many ways, but sadly passed away before the completion of the project. Charlie Bulmer also deserves special mention, for his willingness to find answers to questions, provide clarification, and read numerous revisions of the manuscript. The support for the project of past presidents Tony Edgington and Noel Cleland, as well as others, is much appreciated. Finally, the dedication of Emily (Babs) MacInnes on the administrative, research, and word processing side of the project is gratefully acknowledged.

As the Sproule company approaches its fiftieth anniversary, I am reminded of the company's roots. I don't believe in resting on one's laurels, but I do believe that even while one is focused intently on the future, one should not neglect to respect one's past.

J. Glenn Robinson
President of Sproule Associates Limited

THE SPROULE CHRONOLOGY

1905   John Campbell (Cam) Sproule is born in Edmonton, Alberta.

1927   Cam spends his first season in the field with the Geological Survey of Canada.

1930   Cam earns his B.Sc. from the University of Alberta.

1935   Cam earns his Ph.D. from the University of Toronto and marries Harriet Maude Riley.

1939   Imperial Oil hires Cam to head up their Saskatchewan exploration program.

1946   Cam is appointed senior advisory geologist to International Petroleum in Toronto and works for them in South America.

1951   Cam and his family return to Calgary and Cam establishes consultancy, J. C. Sproule.

1957   Cam is elected president of the Alberta Petroleum Engineers Association.

1958   Sproule is appointed technical advisor to The Borden Royal Commission on Energy.

1959   Cam is elected president of the Canadian Institute of Mining and Metallurgy.

1960   J. C. Sproule and Associates Ltd. is incorporated.

1960   Cam has his new office, "the Bow Building," built at 1009 Fourth Avenue SW.

1960   Filing commences on permits for Arctic Islands acreage.

1963   Cam becomes the first Canadian president of the American Association of Petroleum Geologists.

1966   Panarctic Oils Ltd. is incorporated by Cam Sproule and Eric Connelly.

1966   Northward Aviation, Sproule's airline to the north, is created.

1967   Cam receives the Julian C. Smith medal from the Engineering Institute of Canada.

1967   Arthur Laing announces the federal government's investment in Panarctic Oils Ltd. to the House of Commons, and Dome Petroleum becomes operator; Cam is granted a "net carried interest."

1968   *Oilweek* magazine honours Cam as "Man of the Year."

1968   Cam receives APEGGA's Alberta Centennial Award.

1969   Greenarctic Consortium is formed to explore Greenland's resources.

1970   Cam receives an honourary degree of science from the Notre Dame University in Nelson, B.C.

1970   Cam dies suddenly in Jasper, Alberta, May 21.

1970   Tony Edgington becomes president of Sproule.

1971   Sproule Peninsula, Melville Island, is named after Cam Sproule.

1972   The John Campbell Sproule Memorial Plaque is created by the CIM.

1974   The company name is changed to Sproule Associates Limited.

1976   Sproule relocates to the Alberta Wheat Pool Building.

1980   Northward Aviation folds.

1983   Noel Cleland becomes president when Tony Edgington steps down.

1984   The company moves to the Sun Life Building.

1985   Al Gorrell dies in hotel fire in Manila, Philippines while on assignment for Sproule.

1992   Glenn Robinson becomes president when Noel Cleland steps down.

1992   The company lands its first project in China, working for the Sichuan Petroleum Administration.

1994   Cam's wife, Maude, dies at age 85.

1995   Sproule International Limited is incorporated as a wholly owned subsidiary, headquartered in Calgary.

1997   Sproule Associates Inc. is incorporated as a wholly owned subsidiary, headquartered in Denver, Colorado.

PROLOGUE

Almost fifty years ago, a man whose name was destined to be recognized around the world arrived with his family in Calgary. His name was John Campbell Sproule, an Alberta-born geologist who had already spent twenty years of his career practicing his trade. "Cam" was where he wanted to be—in the heart of Canada's oil industry following the frenzy of the Leduc discovery. He was by all appearances an exploration geologist, but those who knew him saw much more. He was a man with unfettered imagination and vision, and the drive and tenacity to pursue his dreams. He was a man of conviction and integrity, demanding of himself and others, yet highly respected and admired. He would lead the oil and gas industry into the Canadian Arctic, and make Panarctic Oils a reality. Most important, he would build the foundation for a leading petroleum geology and engineering consulting company.

The teaberry provides a vivid contrast against the grey Arctic rock. Photo provided by Sproule Associates.

PIONEER TO OIL MAN

THE EARLY YEARS OF JOHN CAMPBELL SPROULE

*We will not have justified our existence on earth if we
do not leave it a better place for our having lived here.*

Cam Sproule

*The Firebag River, a tributary of the Athabasca River, wends its way
through northeastern Alberta. Photo provided by Sproule Associates.*

Growing Up in Peace River Country

At the turn of the twentieth century, Albert Sproule was a dentist in Westbrook, Nova Scotia with a dream of farming in the Canadian West. In 1904, he left Atlantic Canada with his wife, Agnes, and two-year-old son, Donald, and headed for Alberta to fulfill that dream. The family first settled in Edmonton, where Albert continued to practice dentistry and where son John Campbell (Cam) and daughter Dorothy were born, in 1905 and 1908 respectively. In 1911, Albert turned his attention to a new settlement located in Peace River country, and he gathered up his wife and three children and made the difficult trek along the Edson Trail from Edmonton to Grande Prairie. Considered aristocratic by others on the trail, he drove teams of horses rather than oxen; there were 200 to 300 teams doing the trek that winter. It took the Sproules six weeks to reach their destination, travelling over 500 miles in temperatures dipping to -50°F.

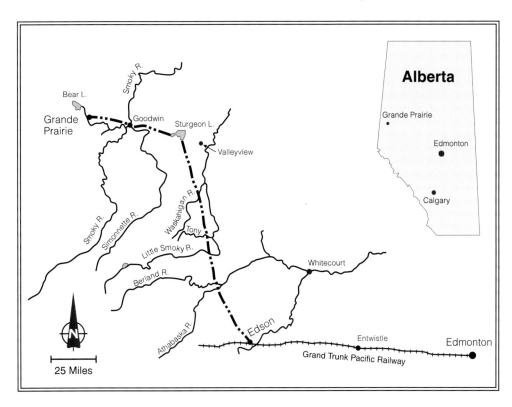

The Edson Trail, 1911–1916.

> He loaded a sleigh with a flat rack to carry a year's provisions, a few pieces of furniture, his professional equipment and, with an eye to filing on a homestead, farm machinery. On another sleigh, he piled his wife Agnes Lillian, their sons Donald Orr and John Campbell and their three year old daughter Dorothy into a canvas covered caboose used for cooking and sleeping on the Long Trail. *(Pioneers of the Peace, 1975)*

According to Cam's daughters, Judy Sproule and Anne McKenzie, their grandfather hated dentistry and planned to give up his practice to work on his homestead. But to Albert's disappointment, the people of the Grande Prairie community needed him. "Albert *had* to do his dentistry," said Anne. "He had no choice."

> When people found out he was a dentist, they would land on his doorstep in a snowstorm at three o'clock in the morning with tooth problems, and whoever was at the door had to live with the family until the storm was over.

Even after the Sproules moved back to Edmonton many years later, Albert made trips to Peace River country to attend to his former neighbours. Good dentists were apparently hard to find—and a good dentist he was. In 1961, when Judy was working for the Victorian Order of Nurses, she visited the home of Fred Parker, a former Calgary teacher who had a school named after him. He was in his late 70s or early 80s at the time, and when he learned her name, he asked her if she was related to Dr. Sproule from Nova Scotia. "He hauled out his teeth and said, 'Your grandfather made these teeth. They're wonderful teeth. I've never replaced them.'"

Because Albert's days were often filled with attending his patients, Agnes (more commonly known as Peggy) and the children looked after the farm. Cam was part of a family living in a community of pioneers, and daily lives were ruled by harsh weather, hard work, and sacrifice. Young and old alike were required to do their share of farm chores, and Cam also helped out with finances by delivering newspapers in his "spare" time. Apparently Cam's older brother, Donald, was considered the most brilliant child in the family, and was allowed to spend his spare time in other pursuits, such as conducting physics experiments in the basement. A certain amount of sibling rivalry arose from Donald's preferential treatment, but ultimately it worked in Cam's favour, because at school, and later university, he was driven to prove he was as talented academically as his big brother.

Working on the farm could hardly have been drudgery for young Cam because he had a great passion for the outdoors. His favourite books were the *Boys Own Adventures* series, which he read voraciously on long, cold winter nights; they inspired his lifelong desire for adventure. "He always felt he was a minuscule part of a great and fascinating world," said Judy. With this sense of self, he developed a burning need to do something of consequence with his life, something that would make a mark and would leave the world a better place than he found it. His love of nature stayed with him all his life. He developed a great respect for living things, both plants and animals, and a thirst for knowledge of everything around him. He was an avid collector; his collections of birds' eggs, butterflies, and stamps survive today.

Convinced that nature was all-powerful, Cam knew that only the strongest would survive, and he revered those who later worked for him in northern Canada who relished the harsh, spartan daily existence of life in the bush. They lived up to the high standards he had set for himself many years before and never wavered from throughout his life.

Albert and Peggy Sproule pose with sons Donald and Cam (sitting) and daughter Dorothy. Photo provided by the Sproule family.

From his parents, Cam learned early the difference between right and wrong. Albert and Peggy had strong moral and religious convictions, and Cam went to the United Church twice every Sunday when he was a boy. He became a man of integrity and principle, which influenced every aspect of his life—personal, social, and business.

Another legacy of Cam's youth was his intolerance for waste: he did not believe in throwing anything away. His daughters recalled how they would sit fascinated, their mother horrified, while he sucked the marrow from the bones of a chicken. When it was time for them to clean their rooms, he stood on guard by the garbage cans and evaluated every item discarded, usually retrieving most and admonishing them for throwing perfectly good things away.

Despite the ongoing rivalry between him and his brother, Cam believed family was one of the most important institutions in society, and that loyalty to one's family was a top priority. In later years, when so much of his time was spent in the field, he corresponded with his wife and daughters regularly, and he took care of his mother's and father's finances as they grew older. Likewise, his younger sister, Dorothy, was greatly loved and looked after by her brothers. Cam, in fact, helped to pay her way through university.

Cam's parents were both university graduates, as were *their* parents. In the days when few boys went to college, and even fewer girls, all three children—Donald, Dorothy, and Cam—completed a post-secondary degree at the University of Alberta (U of A). All graduated with honours and were offered scholarships for post-graduate work. Dorothy went to the McGill School of Social Work in Montreal, and it seems Donald's early experiments paid off: he went to England to study physics and chemistry at the London School of Economics. He eventually became involved in radar work during World War II, and was credited with perfecting a new air echo altimeter, which measured the altitude of a plane in feet every second. His "invention" proved invaluable in making air transport safer, especially at night and in inclement weather.

Cam sits on the shoulders of a classmate, already a head above the rest. Photo provided by Jean O'Brien.

University Days

By 1925, the Sproules had moved from Grande Prairie back to Edmonton, and Cam enrolled at the U of A. He had earned money for college by working for local farmers and as a dental technician for his dad. It was his intention to enroll in medicine, but he said later he could not afford the fees, so he chose geology instead. According to his daughters, their father was a frustrated doctor most of his life, practicing his "quackery" on himself and everyone else. When they were children, the girls were given a glass of "hyposulphite of soda" (a fixing agent used in photography) whenever they were ill. This concoction, Cam's father swore, had cured all the citizens of Grande Prairie during the 1913 flu epidemic. Cam's closest friend and hunting buddy, physician John Noakes, said Cam gargled with the fluid whenever he had a sore throat; clearly he swore by the old-time remedy.

Whether or not Cam really favoured medicine over geology, his interest in geology was aroused in August 1925 when he found a handful of gold nuggets along the Peace River. Cam told *Oilweek* (January 8, 1968) that the river that day was the lowest it had been in about 25 years, exposing numerous sink-holes. He reasoned that if gold nuggets had bounced along the river bottom, they might well have become trapped in the sink-holes: "I reached into one, and pulled out a handful of gravel and several gold nuggets." His plan was to keep his strike quiet until he had a chance to do some prospecting. He put the nuggets back into the sink-hole, thinking it would be as safe a place as any to keep them. The next day, he hiked back to the site. But the river, fed by mountain flash-floods, had risen suddenly overnight, and the sink-holes had been covered with 14 feet of water. "The river has never been that low since, and I guess the gold must still be there."

Cam launched into his geology studies at the U of A with great enthusiasm. He wasted no time joining the Mining and Geological Society and was praised by them in the university's yearbook, *Evergreen and Gold*, for saving the society from enormous losses in oil stock speculation; he had provided a timely discussion of the quality of some of Alberta's oil fields. The Society, organized in 1914, was one of the first mining organizations in northern Alberta. It was affiliated with the Canadian Institute of Mining and Metallurgy (CIM), and those students interested in geology or mining could join the CIM for a reduced fee. (Cam would become the organization's president in 1959.)

Cam graduated from the U of A in 1930 with a Bachelor of Science degree. In the yearbook for that year, he was described in these glowing terms: "If you want to see brains, brawn, sportsmanship and industry in the correct proportions, vide John Campbell."

Adventure awaits; Cam graduates from the University of Alberta in 1930. Photo provided by the Sproule family.

Cam had put himself through university doing odd jobs. Beginning in 1927, he worked during the summer months for the Geological Survey of Canada (GSC). His first job was as a student assistant with the Canadian Topographical Survey in the Babine Mountains of northwestern British Columbia. The assignment was perfect: exploring the countryside by pack-horse and on foot, and sleeping under the stars. He was advised by his boss, John Macdonald, to bring along heavy socks and two pairs of heavy hobnailed boots. Whether or not Cam used the boots that summer is not known. As so many of his colleagues recalled, while everyone else wore heavy boots in the field, Cam ran from outcrop to outcrop, in very rough terrain, wearing his "signature" canvas sneakers.

In 1928, summer work took him to southern Saskatchewan; in the following two years he worked in the Rocky Mountain foothills of southern Alberta. George Hume, renowned GSC geologist, hired him for the foothills work. He described Cam as "extremely energetic and ambitious, with a good undergraduate knowledge of geology—a pleasing personality and a general favourite."

Cam had found his calling. He wasted no time moving on after graduation to the University of Toronto (U of T) to author his Master's thesis. While working on his thesis, he was employed as a research assistant in the Department of Geology.

In the summer of 1931, Cam was placed in charge of a sub-party for the Mines Branch of Canada's Department of Mines and Resources, on a reconnaissance survey of the McMurray asphalt deposit in northern Alberta (more commonly known as the Athabasca tar sands). He worked under Sidney Ells and was responsible for collecting and examining all samples of ancient rocks in the area. At the end of the project, he assisted Ells in producing a report on the tar sands for the Branch.

Cam told *Oilweek* (January 8, 1968) that he covered a lot of ground that summer, sometimes carrying as much as 200 pounds on his back. As a result, his lower spine was injured, "which produced a swelling the size of a potato and which I bandaged up with moss and an old rag." Cam also said he had recently found out that his spine was actually bent as a result. "If I'd know that all along, I might have died from worry."

Cam's interest in the tar (oil) sands continued throughout his life, and the 1931 report was not the last of his writings on the subject. In September 1938, his paper entitled *Origin of McMurray Oil Sands, Alberta* was published in the Bulletin of the American Association of

Petroleum Geologists (AAPG). He concluded that the oil had migrated into the Cretaceous sands from underlying Paleozoic rocks. The paper stimulated much discussion, as evidenced by the published commentary. Although not all the commentators agreed with his conclusion, his efforts at drawing together various geological theories on the origin of the deposits were appreciated. Walter Kupsch, respected academic and consultant for Sproule in the early 1960s, wrote in Cam's obituary that Cam's proposition had become widely accepted.

In 1932, Cam was promoted to demonstrator in the U of T's geology department. In the summer of that year, he worked with the GSC once again, this time in southeastern Ontario. By 1933, he was a full-fledged university instructor working on his Ph.D. degree. He completed his thesis in two years, under the supervision of W.A. Park, professor of paleontology and stratigraphy. The subject of his research was the Cobourg Formation, a geological structure located in Ontario and New York. In the summer of 1934, he tried something new: he signed on with the Ontario Bureau of Mines and worked in the Burntbush River area of northern Ontario.

The following year, on May 15, 1935, at 4:00 P.M., Cam received his degree of Doctor of Philosophy. Still working as an instructor, Dr. Sproule was making $1,500 per year. His degree would not be his only achievement that year. In September, he married a woman whom he had met eight years earlier when both were students at the U of A. His bride was Harriet Maude Riley (Maude), the only daughter of Calgary's Captain Harold Riley and his wife Maude Keene.

The Rileys were Calgary pioneers who, like their son-in-law, believed in making a difference. Harold was the son of Thomas Riley, one of seven brothers who homesteaded on Calgary's north hill. Harold was a Captain in World War I, the first Deputy Provincial Secretary of Alberta, and First Registrar of the University of Alberta. He was a Calgary city alderman for six terms, and an organizer of the Southern Alberta Old Timers' Association. His wife was a well-known Calgary school teacher. In 1918, she founded the Alberta Council on Child and Family Welfare; she remained president for nearly 40 years. As outspoken as Harold was quiet, she worked tirelessly throughout her life for the benefit of Calgary's less fortunate families.

Jean Suitor, Cam's cousin and his bride's best friend, remembered the younger Maude as a "very, very clever girl," who, after graduating from the U of A in 1930, studied French at the University of London in England and the Sorbonne in Paris, on an Imperial Order of the Daughters of the Empire scholarship.

Proud mother Peggy Sproule poses with son Cam.
Photo provided by the Sproule family.

Cam was always serious about Maude, from the first time he set eyes on her. She was beautiful to look at and had a very outstanding personality. She was not a run-of-the-mill person. If she felt like yodelling in the middle of the street, she did. She was very uninhibited. I think he adored Maude because she was full of fun.

Immediately following the wedding at St. Barnabas Church in Calgary, Cam and Maude left by train for Toronto, where Cam returned to his teaching post at the university. However, his life as an academic was about to end. In March 1936, he accepted a full-time position with the GSC in Ottawa. "The idyllic life mother had envisioned," said daughter Judy, "that of a University of Toronto professor and his blue-stockinged bride, was shattered after one year." That life would have suited Maude perfectly, herself an academic, but her husband could not bear "the stuffiness of university life."

GSC Field Man

Once he began with the GSC, Cam was away about seven months of the year, working with various field parties. It was a standing joke in their home, recalled Judy: "When they were married my father pronounced to my mother, 'I'll never leave you, Maude,' and then proceeded to do so!" Maude, however, soon had her hands full taking care of two young children. In 1936, their first child, Anne, was born in Toronto; followed two years later by Judy, who was born in Ottawa.

Cam stayed with the GSC until 1939, working in areas such as Taber, Alberta; Chibougama, Quebec; Cree Lake, Saskatchewan; and Cobequid, Nova Scotia. Judy said her parents wrote each other every day. "They were wonderful letters full of love, loneliness, stories, politics, family doings, and jokes. There is even one Pop wrote on a piece of birch-bark in pencil. His letters to all of us were signed 'Pop the Weasel.'" Anne recalled that when she was two, her father came home after completing his fieldwork in Nova Scotia and said to her, "Hi, I'm your father," to which she replied, "You're not my father—my father is in Nova Scotia."

Cam had a high regard for the GSC, but after a few years it was time to move on. He and Maude were having difficulty making ends meet on the salary provided to him. Not only did they have two children, they were also helping to care for Cam's father, his mother having passed away in 1934. Career-wise, Cam knew his interests in oil exploration could never be satisfied doing GSC work. He had to get involved in the oil industry itself, and take advantage of the opportunities it offered.

There was a young man from Grande Prairie
Who of ladies most always was wary
Till one day he got hooked
and His goose it got cooked
By a Sassy young gal from Calgary.

Maude Sproule

10

Cam had written to Oliver Hopkins, chief geologist at Imperial Oil in Toronto, in 1936, asking for industry work, and to Ted Link, Imperial's chief geologist in Calgary, in 1938. He was ultimately offered a position by "Jimmie" Wheeler, chief geologist of International Petroleum, a subsidiary of Imperial. It was April 1939, and Cam was to report to Saskatchewan. The well-respected Link became Cam's boss.

Although Cam's entry into the oil industry filled him with great excitement, it brought sadness to Maude. She hated to leave Toronto and their many friends. One of Judy's strongest childhood memories is of her mother sitting on their trunks, crying. "For mother, the whole idea of moving was not an adventure." However, there was no question that Maude would follow Cam wherever he went. Theirs was, by all accounts, a dedicated and loving partnership.

Cam was often away more than he was at home, but his children remember him being a wonderful and loving father. He was always at home for Christmas and other special occasions. One Halloween, he designed and made Anne a costume himself. Every winter, Cam built a skating rink for the girls in the backyard. In the summer, when their father was away, their mother had them dig a "hole to China." Judy and Anne spent their summers digging farther and farther down, in the hopes of arriving in that far-away land. "We never did make it," laughed Judy.

> We would get exhausted and make a house instead, filling the hole with all the junk we could drag in. On moving days, father could always be found filling in the hole. It was a long time before I realized that those holes were mother's way of keeping us busy during her long and lonely summers.

According to Judy and Anne, as teenagers they were known to have the strictest father around. "If *we* were allowed to do anything, anyone could." As far as dating was concerned, Judy recalled, Cam told his girls, "There's a wolf behind every bush!"

> He spent agonizing hours checking parked cars in the driveway with a flashlight; gardening in the pitch dark when we entertained a boy in the rumpus room; or standing at the door at midnight, looking at his watch and terrifying the poor, hapless fellow who brought us home.

Cam and Maude take the girls on a family outing to Sulphur Mountain, Banff. Anne is on the left; Judy sits between her parents. Photo provided by the Sproule family.

Searching for Oil on the Saskatchewan Prairie

In the mid-1930s, Canada had only three known major oil reserves: the Norman Wells field in the Northwest Territories, the McMurray oil sands in northern Alberta, and the Turner Valley field in southern Alberta. It was believed that the West held the greatest promise, but Saskatchewan had yet to be fully explored. In the thirties, very little was known about the province from an oil and gas standpoint, except for some gas production around Kamsack and Lloydminster. Between 1919 and 1939, a number of holes had been drilled in North Dakota, in the United States portion of the large Williston Basin. This drilling caught Imperial Oil's attention, and they decided to embark in 1939 on an extensive exploration program in the Saskatchewan area of the Basin, concentrating primarily in the area south of Moose Jaw to the United States border.

For exploration purposes, Imperial incorporated a subsidiary called Norcanols Oil and Gas Company, and used it to take out permits covering several million acres on Crown lands they wished to explore. But Imperial needed a senior earth scientist to take control of exploration. Cam Sproule fit the bill and was made chief geologist. He reported to Saskatchewan in May 1939, arriving at Carlyle Lake with his family, pulling Albert Sproule's old dentistry trailer. Life was pretty rough compared to Toronto. Judy remembered sleeping on straw beds in a house with no plumbing, and watching her mother haul water in pails every day. It was not until Imperial's office was set up in Moose Jaw that the family had a real home in which to live. Nevertheless, Anne said her mother was never offended by their hard life in Saskatchewan, despite having grown up in a well-to-do household with a maid. "She would have done anything for father. I remember them making jokes about having to chop a hole through the ice in the toilet water or the dog's dish." Both daughters remembered Maude cursing about how dry and dusty it was in the summer. Saskatchewan was definitely not one of her favourite places.

In 1940, an Imperial Oil office was established in Moose Jaw, and surface geologists and paleontologists were hired to analyze core samples. Surface surveys proved unfruitful because there were very few outcroppings: a heavy layer of glacial drift (soil, clay, gravel, etc.) covered the bedrock. By the end of 1940, the surface geological parties were joined by drillers, a gravity meter crew, and a seismograph party.

Cam favoured the core drilling process over gravity meter and seismograph, and was particularly interested in microfossils located in the Bearpaw Formation. The paleontologists, who examined the fossils, were also known as "bug pickers." Jack Porter, a student at the time, worked for Sproule during his summer holidays. He remembered who the best bug picker *really* was:

> Through a series of washing and panning with a gold pan, the microfossils were loosened up and the bugs were picked out with the aid of a toothbrush. The bugs were then mounted on a cardboard with round holes, according to their own specific fauna. If there was one that nobody could identify, they would go into Cam's office—he was invariably able to find the appropriate specimen and name it.

Cam's bug pickers paid particular attention to the bugs found in the top of the Bearpaw, which was a Mesozoic marine shale that proved to be the only reliable reference datum. The bugs picked from the Bearpaw Formation served as a reference for regional geological mapping; that is, for determining structural correlations in and between the subsurface rocks.

Although the cores and cuttings were described by the geologists out at the well site, and telephone and written reports were forwarded daily and weekly to Cam, he apparently often re-did the work himself when the samples arrived in Moose Jaw.

Because of Imperial's determination to find oil in Saskatchewan, it was a very hands-on operation. Oliver Hopkins, Jimmie Wheeler, and Ted Link made numerous trips to Moose Jaw and out to the field to see for themselves how things were going. When surface exploration was not getting them results, they ordered gravimetric and seismic surveys.

By the end of 1941, almost 11 million acres had been examined by gravity meter (which determines the density of subsurface rocks at a certain point by the pull of gravity measured at that point). Seismic survey (which measures subsurface rock structures by sound waves bouncing off the rock) came into the works toward the end of 1940. The work in Saskatchewan was done by the Carter Oil Company (a United States-based company) under the supervision of Clare Hurry. The survey conducted was extensive, covering all Norcanols' permits and Imperial Oil's reservations.

Apparently Cam only embraced the seismic information if it fit in with his structure maps. According to William Sanderson, who worked for Imperial as a seismic shot-hole locater, the Carter seismic crew would leave time-depth maps with Cam and let him do his own interpreting. Cam, understandably, would have preferred to rely on his own work and what he had faith in: core samples and the maps produced from the information the samples provided.

Frank Roberts, who was Hurry's "computer," said Cam was very learned, very fair, and very competent. Others that worked with Sproule in Saskatchewan from 1939 to 1945 remember

> *There once was a queerie named Sproule*
> *Whose finances were in a big HOLE*
> *Till one day in a ditch*
> *He struck it so Rich*
> *That he now spends*
> *His life on the DOLE.*
>
> *Maude Sproule*

him as a unique and impressive person, a real leader, who "ran a good show." Some found him demanding to the extreme, a characteristic not unfamiliar to many he worked with throughout the years. Those same individuals said Cam was so hard working and so conscientious, they felt they could not live up to his expectations. He set very high standards for himself, and believed that everyone around him should do the same. Right or wrong, this attitude ensured that Cam always got the most out of his crews, no matter what the task, and in general, those that worked for him greatly respected him and his operation.

Ruby Leon Carter, who worked the drilling rigs in Saskatchewan during Cam's tenure with Imperial Oil, remembered him being somewhat absent-minded. "He took us out to dinner to the house one night. We got there and walked right in the door, and Cam said to the woman of the house, 'What in the hell are you doing here?' She said, 'I live here.' He had sold the house, moved to another one and forgotten all about it." Those who knew Cam might attribute this not so much to absent-mindedness but to his being so busy and preoccupied that he simply forgot some of life's more mundane realities.

Despite Cam's hard work and that of his employees, all 13 holes drilled between 1943 and 1945 were dry. Cam was convinced there was oil to be found, but even his strong convictions could not make it so. Imperial's Williston Basin exploration program came to an end in 1945. Although they had no success finding oil, the main impetus for leaving was the action taken by the government of Tommy Douglas and the Co-operative Commonwealth Federation (the CCF), later known as the New Democratic Party (NDP). An expropriation clause had been added to the Mineral Resources Regulations that essentially allowed the government to expropriate vital industry assets. Fearing expropriation of their properties, oil companies wasted no time in getting out of the province, Imperial Oil included. In fact, attempts were made by the government to expropriate Imperial's refinery in Regina. Frank Roberts remembered Cam calling him on the telephone and asking him to discreetly load up all the office files into his car and drive to the Alberta border, where one of Cam's party chiefs would meet him. Meanwhile, all field equipment was to be moved to Provost, Alberta.

Cam's comments some 20 years later to *Oilweek* (September 28, 1964) indicated that it was not only the policies of the CCF government that led to Imperial's departure from Saskatchewan, but the predominance of geophysics in the program. In the early 1940s, "seismography was all-powerful in the exploration departments of the industry, and as a consequence geologists were out-voted."

> I have a great respect for geophysics as a geological exploration tool as long as it is treated as such. When physicists and mathematicians attempt to interpret their own results, however, they frequently discredit their own work.

In Cam's opinion, presumably, equal emphasis should have been placed on the information derived from the core drilling program.

Although there is no doubt that Cam and everyone within the Imperial organization were disappointed with the outcome of their Saskatchewan exploration program, the work was not without value. First, the geological information showed every known field trend in southern Saskatchewan. Imperial Radville No. 1 (one of the 13 deep tests drilled during the 1939–1945 program) not only suggested the possibility of commercial oil production from the Mississippian carbonates (the Mississippian spans 345–320 million years ago), it also encountered rich potash beds in the Middle Devonian (the Devonian spans 400–345 million years ago). The highly successful potash industry was established in Saskatchewan several decades later.

Perhaps most important, Imperial Oil moved its field office to Edmonton, and the Leduc oil field was discovered in 1947. The official word from Imperial was that the disappointing search for oil in Saskatchewan led them straight to Leduc: it was the seismic parties who had just completed their work in Saskatchewan that came to Alberta and found the Leduc field.

As for Cam, he wrote an excellent report summarizing the southern Saskatchewan exploration program that, according to Henry Sawatzky, a geophysicist who worked for the Saskatchewan Department of Mineral Resources, "ranked head and shoulders above any other assessment reports submitted."

> Without subtracting from the value of the work done by explorationists such as R. L. Milner with the Tidewater Group and R. A. Bishop with Sohio during the 1950s, it was the Sproule reports that hinted at the major role that the dissolution of Middle Devonian salt and subsequent collapse of overlying beds played in the configuration of the Saskatchewan subsurface sediments.

> It was the structure test-hole program supervised by Cam that first indicated the pronounced folding and faulting of the shallow bedrock exposed in the Dirt Hills area near the village of Avonlea, Saskatchewan. This disturbance was not manifested in the subsurface below the Cretaceous Bearpaw

---

The Radville Song

Cam's daughter Judy recalled a song her mother used to sing to her father, to the tune of "I've been working on the railroad":

> *Daddy's got a hole in Radville*
> *Ninety miles away—*
> *Daddy's got a hole in Radville*
> *And he goes there every day—*
> *Can't you see the oil a-blow'n*
> *Up and down that hole,*
> *Can't you hear the oil a-blow'n*
> *And it blows right over Sproule!*

And when her mother was really mad at him, Judy said she would sing "water" instead of "oil." "The Radville song was 'pure mother.'"

Formation. The reports suggested that the near-surface disturbances were the result of "ice push" processes during the Pleistocene ice age when the shallow bedrock behaved like crystalline rock because of the permafrost.

The concepts mentioned above were reluctantly accepted by traditional thinkers in later years and certainly facilitated the proper interpretation of many Saskatchewan subsurface problems.

Sojourn in South America

By the spring of 1945, Cam was back in Calgary as head of Imperial Oil's subsurface department. However, it was not long before he was transferred to International Petroleum's offices in Toronto. He was chief geologist, and part of his mandate was to take on exploration work in South America. This was undoubtedly an exciting prospect, not only because of the country's diverse geology, but because of the opportunity to explore new terrain, encounter unique wildlife, and experience a very different culture.

The Sproules lived in Toronto for over a year before heading to South America, though Cam made preliminary trips to Colombia in the fall of 1946. As always, Cam's time in Toronto was memorable. Jean Greig, Imperial's librarian at the time, remembered him "going through the place like a strong wind." She found Cam frustrating at times, "but it was impossible to stay mad at him, because he was basically a very nice, and decent, person."

Cam was infamous for his driving habits, not only in Toronto, but everywhere he lived, and Jean remembered him driving her home from the office one evening.

> I had no worries about his ability as a driver—he manoeuvred like crazy. I was afraid not that we'd have an accident, but that we'd get arrested before we even got to Queen's Park. He would cut from lane to lane whenever he saw an opening. I was just holding my breath a lot of the time. But we got home without incident, a lot of swearing drivers left in our wake.

Cam's travel itinerary was dated August 25, 1947. He and his family flew to New York from Toronto, and after spending four exciting days in that city, they sailed with their beloved dog Boopsey to South America, on a route that would take them through the Panama Canal. "For Pop it must have been an episode right out of his *Boys Own Adventures*," said Judy. They passed through the Panama Canal in the middle of the night, and Judy remembered her father being very excited, trying to wake up her, Anne, and her mother so they could witness the event. He was most exasperated when he was unable to stir them from their berths.

Cam's first assignment in South America was in Peru. He was to be chief geologist in Lima, with a salary of $12,500 per year. Soon after the family's arrival, Cam was whisked off to the field. Anne and Judy remembered that at each of their postings—first Lima and Talara in Peru, and then Bogota, Colombia—their father was away most of the time. (He also spent field time in Venezuela and Ecuador.) Nevertheless, his daughters have wonderful memories of his stories and of events that occurred during their stay.

On one occasion, their father came home with a large snake fang embedded in his calf. The girls watched in fascination and horror as he squeezed it from his leg without a hint of squeamishness. Not only did he bring back tribal head-dresses, poisoned arrows, and

Imperial Oil "sends off" their chief geologist to South America. Left to right at the head table: Marg and Ernie Shaw, Cam and Maude, Stan Harding. Photo provided by Clark Siferd.

snake skins from his field trips, he once brought home two spider monkeys from the jungle. Maude walked around with one on each foot so they could keep warm while they adjusted to the cooler temperatures of Lima.

Life in South America was not without danger. There were natives who, although friendly by day, practiced cannibalism at night. Cam lost a friend to drowning when their canoe was caught in a whirlpool and he also escaped death when he missed a flight that subsequently crashed, killing everyone on board. It was not just Cam who could encounter danger at any time: the whole family saw locals being fired upon by police, and there were many afternoons when Maude was sick with worry, waiting for her young daughters to return home from school.

In Bogota, Cam was assigned to geologist Jack Browning's field party. Jimmie Wheeler and Chris Dohm (chief geologist for Tropical Oil Company, International Petroleum's South American subsidiary), thought Cam would most benefit from his time in Colombia if he was initially assigned to a seasoned party chief. After he became acquainted with the area, local customs, and language, he would be ready to head up his own party.

Cam was excited about the posting to Colombia, wanting to learn as much as possible about strata deposited during the Tertiary period (the Tertiary spans 65–2 million years ago). He was able to use his expertise in photogrammetry on this assignment, having a complete collection of air photos and mosaics from Peru. Cam had asked to join Browning's field party in particular, as he had worked with him in Moose Jaw.

Browning, who became a good friend of Cam's, said that Cam was of tremendous help to him in planning and geological interpretation. In 1951, Browning turned down Cam's offer of a position in Cam's consultancy. "One of the biggest mistakes of my life," he said.

Cam's time with Browning's field party was well spent. The parties in Colombia were quite different from what he had been accustomed to. Crews were extremely large and the logistics of moving every two to three days, without interfering with the fieldwork, was difficult. In addition, the party chief was responsible for hiring, firing, managing payroll, helping locals with health concerns, purchasing food, etc.

After training with Browning, Cam was assigned his own party. His reputation as an intense and hard-working geologist preceded him. Geologist Warren Henker was well aware of that reputation.

> What a driver—Sproule worked by example. Everybody had to follow him. He ran between outcrops and waded across streams, the hardest-working field man that the company had ever seen. He was a geologist's geologist, a gentleman's gentleman— friendly, sincere, honest. The last of the Docs.

However, all was not well within Tropical Oil's organization. Browning resigned in 1949 out of frustration and disappointment. Writing to Cam, he complained about "the complete lack of organization in the company," and the fact that he witnessed "one drilling prospect after another discarded through poor technique."

Cam stayed an additional two years with International Petroleum in Toronto. International was ultimately sold by Imperial Oil to Imperial's parent, Standard Oil of New Jersey, to raise funds to develop the Redwater and Leduc fields in Alberta. The sale meant that International Petroleum's headquarters moved from Toronto to Coral Gables, Florida.

In July 1951, Cam was offered a roving commission between Colombia and Peru, a job he said he would have been delighted to take, except that his daughters would have to go to a private boarding school. Cam felt that South America was fine for young children, but not for teenagers. In correspondence to Jimmie Wheeler regarding his decision, he explained this, adding that although Maude had also enjoyed life in South America, she too had no desire to break up the family. In addition, Cam was a Canadian and an ardent nationalist, and wanted to put his expertise to work in his own country.

During his time in Peru and Colombia, Cam learned about many facets of the oil business, including dealing with everyone from drillers to money-men. His experiences proved of great benefit to him in his next endeavour—establishing his own consultancy. Cam planned on returning to Alberta, a logical choice, given the opportunities and excitement Leduc had created throughout the province.

Cam pores over aerial photos in a South American field camp. Jack Browning sits to his right; Paul Taylor faces him. Note Cam's sneakers. Photo provided by Jack Browning.

EXPLORATION TO EVALUATION

THE CONSULTANCY 1951–1970

Any job that is worth doing is worth doing well. We will not accept
any assignment that we are not capable of carrying out properly.

J.C. Sproule and Associates

The Heart Lake Reef towers over the forest of the Hay River area in
the Northwest Territories. Photo provided by Sproule Associates.

Back Home to Booming Alberta

Alberta-born Cam Sproule thought his home province as vital a place to be as any for someone interested in oil exploration. He believed the oil basins in Western Canada could rival those of Venezuela, and did not share the sentiment of some pessimists in the industry who, after Leduc and Redwater, felt that the Alberta "boom" was a bubble soon to burst. On the contrary, Cam thought there was too much value in the ground in the West not to see the situation continuing well into the future. In fact, in a 1952 letter to Imperial Oil employee Bill Denton, a year after arriving in Calgary, he wrote:

> I do think, however, that next summer will see by far the biggest Western Canadian oil boom in history. By that time it will become apparent that it actually is not a "Boom" but a permanent situation. Western Canada will undoubtedly be a great oil producing country within the next few years.

The Sproule family left Toronto for Calgary the last week of August 1951. Ted Link, who was running his own consulting firm in Calgary with Art Nauss, offered Cam temporary office space in his building, so that he could spend his first few weeks getting settled and acquainting himself with the business of consulting.

Cam and Maude purchased an older home in the Mount Royal area of Calgary, and the family lived in the Bluebird Motel on Macleod Trail while the house was remodelled. Cam complained to a friend in Colombia about, "... a gang of Contractors and Carpenters who appear to converge on our house during the bad weather and disappear during the good weather." He hoped to have his family settled in their new home by Christmas.

The Players

It was not long before Cam had his own office space (at 330 Seventh Avenue SW) and hired a secretary. Cam's cousin, Gladys Smith, recommended Willa Tegart, of Toronto, and Cam contacted her by letter September 18, 1951. Willa arrived in Calgary on October 6 (she was paid $250 per month) and became one of Sproule's most valuable employees. Judy Sproule said, "Mother looked after father at home, and Willa looked after father at the office." Willa became known as guardian of the morals around the office; Cam would have

Thin-bedded shale forms the pages of time at the Chinchaga River, northern Alberta. Photo provided by Sproule Associates.

most heartily approved. She ensured the ladies dressed appropriately, and liberties were not taken by the men with respect to expense accounts and days off. She proved more and more valuable to Cam and his company as the years passed.

Settled in his new office with his "gal Friday" at his side, Cam set about hiring the best geologists available. In the early years of J. C. Sproule, the company, in keeping with Cam's vision, focused on providing geological exploration expertise to the oil industry. Although engineers were hired early in the company's history, the engineering side did not predominate until later.

Sproule's first geologist was John Wall [*authors' note: except in some quoted material, Sproule refers to the company, not the man*], who had worked for Cam in Saskatchewan as a "bug picker." He was hired on contract in early 1952 to prepare a set of subsurface contour maps of Alberta using data taken from wildcat wells. In the spring of that year, geologist "Mickey" Crockford became Sproule's first salaried employee. He had worked for California Standard Company (later known as Chevron) after graduating, and then the Research Council and the Oil and Gas Conservation Board. He brought to Sproule extensive and varied experience in stratigraphy, paleontology, geological mapping, and subsurface studies.

Mickey was well liked and was mentor to some of the younger geologists who joined the firm. Initially, his primary job was to supervise fieldwork, which covered locations across Western Canada, from northeastern B.C. to southeastern Manitoba. By 1955, Mickey was almost exclusively involved with subsurface studies; his specialty was natural gas occurrences and reserves. Although he and Cam reportedly clashed at times, Mickey, like Cam, was a field man at heart. Geologist George Furnival, one-time Sproule employee, said Mickey was "a very hard-driving field man." In fact, he was known as "The Iron Man," because none of his assistants could keep up to him; it was no wonder that he was at the top of Cam's list of sought-after employees. Mickey was with Sproule until 1964.

Next to join the company, in 1953, was geologist Stan Harding; like John Wall, he was an Imperial Oil man. In fact, in the first few years of the business, Cam became concerned about Imperial Oil and International Petroleum accusing him of stealing their employees. As it happened, half of Sproule's early employees came from those two companies. But Cam did not want to "step on anyone's toes"; old friends such as Jimmie Wheeler were still with the organization. He admitted that he became "Public Enemy No. 1" in Imperial Oil's Calgary office. Cam's "blacklisting," however, did not keep him from writing his former co-workers and explaining how the West was in need of good technical and production men. From his letter to Mose Knebel, Exploration Co-ordinator for Standard Oil, dated May 8, 1953, Cam's view was clear:

> In case you should get a one-sided impression, I may say that in both cases these men [*probably referring to Stan Harding and Des Boggs (who joined Sproule in 1953)*] were practically lost to Imperial before I entered the picture.

> I may say further, for the sake of my "Alma Mater", that if Imperial don't pay a little more attention to realizing the relative value of their geological staff compared with their geophysical staff, they will lose still more men before the story is told.

Stan had worked for Cam in Saskatchewan right after graduating from the University of Saskatchewan. Cam put him in charge of catching core samples on shot-hole rigs. He continued working for Cam in Saskatchewan, as a wellsite geologist, after completing his Master's degree. When Cam was transferred to Imperial Oil's Calgary office in 1945, prior to going to South America, Stan followed as his assistant.

Cam approached Stan in May 1953. "I had to think pretty hard about it," recalled Stan, "because I felt, rightly or wrongly, that there was a certain amount of security in being with Imperial Oil." But he decided to take the risk and accepted Cam's offer: $10,000 per year plus a 10 percent interest in the profits of the firm.

Stan proved indispensable. Like Willa, he was one of Sproule's most loyal employees, remaining with the company until retiring in 1972. Stan's work at Sproule included supervision of subsurface work and structure test projects, surface geological mapping projects in the Northwest Territories and prairie provinces, fieldwork in the

"You've got five minutes." Photo provided by the Sproule family.

Arctic, and studies on the potash areas of Saskatchewan, Brazil, Poland, and Morocco.

Stan was highly respected by everyone at Sproule. Keith Williams, a senior field geologist hired in 1954, said Stan was key to the organization; everyone trusted and liked him. Cam relied heavily on Stan, not just for his geological expertise, but for his ability to "calm the waters" when things got a little "choppy." Because of his calm, less driven temperament, he often served as mediator between Cam and his employees. Cam was not the easiest person to work for; he could be demanding, unyielding, quick-tempered, and abrupt, and there were times when he alienated his staff. Stan smoothed ruffled feathers, or took on the employee's cause and battled it out with Cam. Stan had open-heart surgery in 1972, the year he retired. Stress was undoubtedly a factor, according to his doctors. "Nineteen years I was with Sproule," said Stan, "and most of the time I was between Sproule and the staff."

Although Stan was hired as an Associate, with an interest in the profits, it was clear that Cam did not wish to operate as a partnership, or share ownership. It took many years and much persistence on the part of his Associates before Cam agreed to give up any interests in the company. In the beginning, all professional employees were simply paid a salary, and a percentage of the profits was paid to Associates—originally Mickey, Stan, and Des Boggs.

Des Boggs was hired about the same time as Stan, in 1953. Des spent some 20 years in Ecuador and Peru working for International Petroleum, so Cam knew him well. Just prior to joining Sproule, Des was working for Imperial Oil in Edmonton. A mining engineer who worked as a geologist, he was in his early sixties when he came to work for Sproule. According to Stan, Des was not eligible for a pension from Imperial because he had worked on and off for them over the years, so the decision to join Sproule was not difficult. Des's primary work at Sproule was reserve estimates and evaluation.

Des worked for Cam for almost ten years. In 1959, he returned to his native Ontario and set up an office in Kettleby, Ontario, where he would remain for a number of years as Sproule's eastern contact and representative. Cam was extremely fond of Des, and when he left for Ontario (with a 70th birthday behind him), Cam instructed him as follows: "You are not obligated to carry out work for us to any greater extent than you see fit to do. The amount of work you engage in is entirely at your own discretion." Keith Williams credited Des with being one of the first to figure out the geology of the Norman Wells field in the Northwest Territories. His work showed the existence of a reef in the area.

Branching Out

In the summer of 1953, geologist Bob Laurence, anxious to try a branch office, set up shop for Sproule in Vancouver, B.C. His mandate was to provide services to anyone interested in Alberta oil development, including anything from purchasing oil royalties to exploring land holdings held in lease or reservation. In addition, the office would accept field mapping and well-servicing assignments in northeastern B.C. However, although there was some interest in oil and gas exploration in Vancouver, it was not enough to justify the existence of an office, and it was closed by April 1954. For a short time, there was also an office in Victoria.

This wasn't to be Sproule's only attempt at a "branch" office. In 1963, Cam made a move to expand to Australia. He sent geologist Jan Bakhoven, who as it happened was travelling to Sydney in May of that year to do some work for a Canadian client. Bakhoven liaised in Sydney with a friend of Cam's, Arthur Lucie-Smith, who Cam knew from his Imperial Oil days. Jan and Arthur opened an office in Sydney and secured a few consulting jobs, but did not find enough work to make the venture economically viable. Bakhoven left Australia the following year, in December 1964, and the office closed shortly after.

In 1964 Sproule also tried a branch office in Chatham, Ontario; Bert Corey was hired to run it. Cam believed the operation would be successful, given the amount of oil and gas exploration that was going on in southwestern Ontario. However, a number of factors necessitated the closing of the office after only a short time. Exploration in the area began to decline, and there wasn't any indication that it would pick up. Corey said that despite efforts at promotion, Sproule was a newcomer in the area, and it was difficult to get clients when there were well-established and competent companies, with more staff, doing the same kind of work. Rather than suffer any further losses, Tony Edgington, chief engineer, advised Cam to give up the office. It closed July 15, 1965.

Not until 1997 did Sproule open another branch office; a new subsidiary was formed, and an office in Denver, Colorado was established.

"Punch" Logan joined the company in 1954—Sproule's first field engineer. The company was doing fieldwork in Saskatchewan at the time, and Punch would spend a large part of his time working on drilling and production operations, often in the Kindersley area. Tony Edgington, fellow engineer and future president of Sproule (he joined Sproule in 1958), joked later, "Punch represented the initial infusion of sanity and reason that naturally accompanies education and experience in engineering." The "friendly feud" between geologists and engineers is one of the more constant elements in Sproule's long history.

A number of others joined the company in the early years. Geologist Rein de Wit joined Sproule in 1957, with experience in stratigraphic studies in Europe and across Canada. Gus Van Wielingen became the company's first gas engineering specialist in 1958. John Maughan was also hired in 1958, to take care of petroleum engineering and related production and drilling engineering services. "These three were added to expand the firm's services, and with a promise of profit sharing," said geologist Charlie Bulmer, who "hired on" in 1955.

> They joined the original three—Stan, Des, and Mickey—and Cam, of course, first as a planning and supervisory group, and then, after incorporation, as an executive committee and directors group. Other than Stan's share [*in 1964*], none of these held shares, although a share distribution was promised.

A group of young professionals who joined the company during the 1950s and 1960s would eventually become Associates and then part of the Executive Committee and Board of Directors. Charlie Bulmer joined the company fresh out of the U of A, spent a few months in the drafting department, then filled a spot in a field party going to the Northwest Territories. He was with Sproule until he retired in 1996, and still consults for the company. Geologist Don Campbell (a cousin to Cam) was hired in 1956 after several summer field seasons with the company while still a student at the U of A. He left Sproule in 1964, but then returned five years later to head surface and photogeological studies. Geologist Al Gorrell was another Imperial Oil alumnus, hired in 1957 to augment the expanding subsurface geological work. Gordon Jones, another geologist, was hired in 1960 to apply his experience as a photogeologist to Sproule's surface geological interpretations. Earl Miller became treasurer in September 1964, after being involved with the company's audit for several years while employed with Price Waterhouse.

Geologist and Potter Team Up

There seemed to be a natural connection between Cam's love of geology and his affection for pottery. In 1952, he decided to provide financial backing to local artist, Luke Lindoe, to start up a ceramics studio in Calgary. They knew each other from Saskatchewan, where Luke had worked with Cam looking for outcrops for Imperial Oil.

Luke was teaching at the Alberta College of Art when Cam approached him. He had, however, become disillusioned, complaining that the college was more interested in teaching students how to be successful, rather than teaching them art. Luke and Cam conceived "Lindoe Studios," later to be known as "Ceramic Arts," Alberta's first commercial ceramics studio.

The studio was set up on land owned by Cam, adjacent to Sarcee Trail, just south of the old Banff Coach Road junction on 53rd Street SW. Luke organized the building of the studio, which included a small apartment and a 40-cubic-foot updraft kiln, the largest in the province at the time. When it opened in 1954, they used mostly casing and drape moulding techniques and did some wheel work. Ashtrays became the studio's stock-in-trade, not necessarily what Luke had envisioned.

In the early days, the studio was a training ground for some of Alberta's major potters, and through the years, most of Alberta's well-known potters were involved in the studio: Walter Dexter, John Porter, Nils Graveson, Les Manning, Vivian Lindoe, Katie Ohe, Jane Van Alderwegen, and Walter and Pat Drohan.

Unfortunately, Luke and Cam did not see eye-to-eye on the direction the ceramics studio would take. Lindoe thought that Cam wanted to have a manufacturing company, but operating in a 50-50 partnership did not suit Cam's needs because, according to Luke, it did not give him the tax dispersal mechanism he needed. Luke was unable to attain his objective of increasing the output of pottery through mass production techniques. In addition, Luke was barely able to take care of himself and his family financially. Much to Luke's frustration, there never was an agreement signed between him and Cam, and Luke left the studio after only two years. Luke moved to Medicine Hat in 1957, where he applied the knowledge he had gained from geological survey work to Medicine Hat's brick and tile industry. The Alberta College of Art honoured Lindoe some years later by naming their library after him. As Luke said, "I've become a folk hero and folk villain."

Ceramic Arts did see success some 14 years later, in 1968, under the direction of John Porter. The studio finally showed some profit, allowing it to continue for a few more years, employing Alberta College of Art students and providing a place where local artists could work. Unfortunately, developers had been eyeing the property for years, given its location on some of Calgary's choicest real estate, and the property was sold in the early 1970s.

Gift Giver

Cam's employees and clients, and virtually anyone associated with him in the 1950s and 1960s, recalls Cam giving them a piece of pottery, usually an ashtray. In 1969, Cam wrote to an acquaintance at the Department of Transport in the Northwest Territories:

> The Ceramic Artists in my shop here are not particularly business-like, as a result of which they only produce more of these hand-made articles when their present stock is gone. In order to keep them busy and 'healthy', therefore, I am my own best customer by removing the produce somewhat like a farmer takes away eggs, so the hens will lay more. I hope you may find some use for these in your office, bar, etc.

Noel Cleland fondly remembered Cam, on one occasion, insulting his Associates on a Friday afternoon with respect to the issue of sharing ownership in the company. Frustrated by Cam's behaviour, they all left work early and went off to a local drinking establishment to commiserate. By way of atonement Monday morning, Cam came into the office bearing a piece of pottery for each of them, probably not the first piece to adorn their offices.

Cam also commissioned specific pieces to be made for special occasions. One such occasion was the birthday of his good friend, Ted Link. Cam presented Ted with a ceramic replica of a pregnant goat. No doubt Ted was very pleased with the gift, as it was a great improvement over the gift Cam presented him with the year before—a live pregnant goat! (Cam thought the animal could save Ted, who had recently moved to Victoria, the trouble of cutting all that green grass!)

Getting Down to Business

Other experienced, hard-working professionals joined the group, and Sproule began concentrating on developing its clientele. Even in the early days, Cam was, by all accounts, a promoter. "There's no room for pessimists in the oil business," geologist Bob Workum remembered him saying. "In fact, not even much room for realists. The oil industry flourishes on optimism!" With the contacts he had made over the previous 20 years, it would not have been difficult for Cam to "round up" clients. In fact, before he had even left Toronto for Calgary, he was writing letters to prospective clients. One of them was to Tidewater Associated Oil Company of Saskatchewan, offering to be their exclusive Saskatchewan consultant. Cam also had a lot of connections in eastern Canada, particularly with the mining companies. Bob remembered Cam going East seeking clients, and coming back with "bags of money" in the form of work contracts.

The 1950s in Alberta were ideal for setting up J.C. Sproule: the province was ripe for individuals and companies interested in oil and gas exploration. Predictably, Cam excelled in the consultancy business. It was partly his ability to attract clients; he seemed to inspire trust. That and his enthusiasm for the work ensured a steady stream of clients in the early years.

The main thrust of the company's work was exploration geology and property evaluations, with some subsurface, wellsite, and production work. They provided recommendations regarding further exploration activities on properties (for example, geophysical studies or drilling), as well as values for those properties after pertinent

Cam consults with two of his senior men. From left: Cam, Tony Edgington, and Al Gorrell. Photo provided by the Sproule family.

data were retrieved. The rapidly expanding engineering department in the late 1950s increased the company's capabilities for estimating oil and gas reserves, preparing production forecasts and cash flows, and determining present worth values.

At the beginning, J. C. Sproule mostly worked locally, for both small companies and "the majors." Their success was due in part to putting senior men on the job, according to Stan Harding:

My experience with Imperial Oil was that you start out in the field, and if you showed some promise you moved to a supervisory position, and in no time at all you were an office man. So the field men were always new. By putting senior men out in the field, Sproule had no problem competing with the majors' own field parties.

Not only did Cam put his senior men in charge of the field parties, he made numerous trips to the field himself. While clients appreciated this hands-on approach, his own employees did not always look forward to his visits. When Cam joined his men in the field, they counted the minutes until his departure, and he left them exhausted. He apparently had phenomenal amounts of energy. "He could not sit still for more than 30 seconds," Keith Williams recalled. "He set a whirl-wind pace during his visits."

Armed with experienced draftsman Gordon McCracken (who Cam knew from his South America days) and an extensive library of aerial photos, Sproule could offer more than their competitors. "In Western Canada," said Don Campbell, "Sproule was a pioneer in photogeology." In the early days, U.S.-based Geo-Photo was apparently the only other company that could compete with Sproule's library of aerial photographs. Cam, himself, had become somewhat of an expert in interpreting aerial photos, after his days in South America.

Aerial photos were invaluable in organizing geological and geophysical exploration programs in Alberta and B.C. because they provided an excellent first view of the survey area. The photos proved indispensable in managing exploration of large reservations involving structure test hole work, geophysical work, subsurface work, and geological mapping.

By the end of the 1950s, Cam had between 60 and 65 employees, including engineers, geologists, draftsmen, photogrammetrists, reproduction clerks, and stenographers, as well as two pilots for fieldwork. The company advertised expertise in reserves evaluation, land evaluation, production forecasts, company evaluation, field reserve studies, gas engineering, geological evaluation of lands and reserves, surface exploration, and photogeological surveys. The vast array of services Sproule offered was critical to their survival in the

Geologists map outcrops in the Pouce Coupe Creek area near Alberta's western border. Photos provided by Lois Harding.

next decade, when Cam's interest in Arctic exploration proved to be very expensive. According to Earl Miller:

> Sproule mounted anywhere from two to four field parties per year during the early 1960s but found it impossible to obtain sufficient paying clients to cover the actual costs. It was estimated that over a five-year period Sproule costs exceeded revenues by over $1 mm, which is probably the equivalent of $10 million in today's terms.

While Cam focused much of his attention on the Arctic, sending geological field parties every summer between 1960 and 1967, local work continued. Sproule not only evaluated proven properties (where reserves of oil and gas are known), but unproven properties as well. At first, Cam assigned values to the latter, using, for the most part, his experience and knowledge. "Cam's numbers were based on his extensive knowledge of the geology of Western Canada," said Charlie Bulmer, "as well as the general knowledge of values of similar lands based on previous sales, the costs of exploration and development, and the value of potential reserves discovered." Charlie recalled that some of Cam's employees thought he picked his numbers out of thin air, because no calculations accompanied them. He would place all the per-acre values on exploratory lands and Willa would faithfully do all the mathematical calculations to arrive at the total estimated values of the properties.

Computer programs and complex methodologies had yet to be developed. Clients, however, gradually became more sophisticated, and began to ask the origin of a given value. So, over a period of time Sproule had to develop methodology for comparing one property to another. Cam used his staff of geologists to do analyses of the local geology to provide a better comparison with value paid for similar properties.

When Charlie was put in charge of the subsurface geological department in January 1969, Jim Chilton was doing most of the "unproven property" pricing, subject to Cam Sproule's approval.

> Since this fell within my responsibility, I recognized that we needed a more precise method of evaluating unproven properties, since we could not count on Sproule's knowledge and experience (and recognition!) to defend our values. I introduced some risk analysis techniques for Jim Chilton to incorporate into the process, and worked with him to create a "work commitment formula" to be used for evaluation purposes, where properties were "farmed out" and the "farmee" earned an interest by paying the cost of some exploratory work. The terms of the farmout arrangement were

---

Cam's Crystal Ball

In 1953, the Cardium pool of the Pembina oil field was discovered. Cam predicted that the field would have 1,000 wells—a prediction that many at the time thought was a ridiculous over-estimate. Cam based his prediction, Charlie Bulmer presumed,

> *on the spacing and distribution of the first number of wells drilled in the pool and with the knowledge of the widespread nature of the Cardium sandstone in the province—from outcrop and well data existing at that time. A widespread stratigraphic trap would lead to that number of producing wells.*

Cam's prediction, in fact, turned out to be a conservative one. By the mid-1960s, there were between 2,950 and 3,000 wells capable of production at Pembina.

used in the formula to arrive at a per-acre value represented by the deal.

Al Gorrell was the main evaluator of unproven properties, followed by Jim Chilton. Jim Terrill took over the task when the latter retired. Currently, geologist Wayne Sargent has that responsibility. "We always believed we had a rather unique service to offer, that no other consulting firm had," said Charlie, "at least with respect to the geological input and methodology."

Part of the risk analysis involved applying an economic program. Sproule had its own economic program since the beginning of the 1960s, one of the first in the industry. Clark Smith worked on it in 1961 using the IBM1620, which was used in reserves evaluations to create present worth values. According to Charlie:

> For evaluating unproven properties, a production profile for anticipated reserves, together with expected oil and gas prices and exploratory development and production costs were entered into the program, which then produced a cash flow and present worth values. An anticipated range of values with assigned probabilities were used in a risk analysis to calculate an "expected monetary value" (or risk-weighted value), which became an estimated value for the property.

Over time, the company accumulated a library of maps with values already derived for various lands, so that many future evaluations for clients could be readily compared to a value already placed on a similar prospect. With continued experience in this process, the geologists developed a sense of a property's value before "running the numbers." Like Cam, they developed a "feel" for the lands based on their own knowledge and experience.

Expert Witness

Sproule's expertise in property evaluation occasionally resulted in its being called upon to provide expert testimony in cases where disputes arose over issues regarding exploration, evaluation, and development of lands. In 1960, Sproule was hired by Scurry-Rainbow Oil to evaluate certain lands of Farmers Mutual Petroleums (a Scurry subsidiary) that were in dispute as a result of alleged breaches on the part of the farmees—the United States Smelting Refining and Mining Company, and Agawam Oil Co. They examined geological and engineering data, which revealed estimates of undeveloped oil reserves at certain dates, and they related those to production taken from adjoining lands. The drainage that had occurred was estimated, and the damages occasioned by the failure to drill offsets were calculated. Sproule had to determine what a reasonable and prudent operator would have done in the way of exploration and development on the subject lands during the period the various parcels were available for development, and then compare it with the actual development done by United States Smelting and Agawam.

His Lordship, Chief Justice Bence of the Court of Queens Bench, Judicial Centre of Regina, commented about Cam's testimony in his judgment given July 20, 1962, two years after Sproule began the project:

> *I was impressed by Sproule's qualifications and the manner in which he gave his evidence. He refused to be drawn into any matters on which he had not made a detailed study and gave his evidence in a careful and considered manner.*

Conversely, with respect to another witness, the Judge wrote, "He was honest but not too certain of his own opinions."

In regard to the Defendants' expert witness, whose evidence was directly contrary to that of the Plaintiff's witnesses, the judge said:

> *I also received the impression throughout the whole of this witness' testimony that he was endeavouring to bolster the Defendants' case at every turn and was willing to concede very little although it was apparent to me in some cases that he should have made concessions.*

In the end, the Judge awarded the Plaintiff, Farmers Mutual, damages for the failure of the Defendant to drill, pursuant to the terms of the development contract.

North of 60

Beginning in the 1950s, Sproule worked in a part of northern Alberta very familiar to Cam—the oil sands area north of Fort McMurray. Stan Harding led the field parties, mapping the Athabasca River and its tributaries and measuring the exposed section of the McMurray Formation. No doubt Cam would never have turned down work in the area, because he believed that the day would come when commercial production from the sands would be economically feasible. He also believed that the sands could be used to produce heavy oil, thus reducing Canada's demand for imports of heavy crude and its by-products.

Beginning in the spring of 1953, Sproule geologists left Calgary and worked through the summer, until September or October. There would have been no complaints made about the lack of comforts of home in the field. In South America, Imperial Oil's geologists, including Cam, were in the field twelve months of the year. Cam's men in Canada had it easy (though their wives may not have thought so): they were only away four to five months, and always home for Christmas.

The first job Sproule took in the Northwest Territories was for Northwest Territories Petroleums. The second was for D. Todd Briggs, an American company, which took them south-west of the Hay River (south of Great Slave Lake), mapping the geology from the river west to Fort Simpson and Fort Liard into Yukon Territory. Before this project, Sproule geologists working on the plains were used to driving trucks and travelling on farmers' roads. The Northwest Territories was a different story—it was the wilderness. No longer would trucks be used—the new method for surveying was by helicopter.

Sproule (Stan Harding in particular) was a pioneer in the use of helicopters for geological surveying. The company chartered a Bell Model D from a company called Canadian Helicopters. Stan remembered flying around with the doors off "the bird," held in by seat belts alone. Using helicopters, when all previously published fieldwork had been done by canoe, was a huge improvement: the whole area and its many geological formations could be mapped. As Stan said, "The helicopter was useful for getting the original picture and tying in the ground geology."

Cam managed the Briggs project himself. The permit area was virgin territory, encompassing four and a half million acres. After doing surface structure mapping work on the permit area, a well was drilled in 1954 at Rabbit Lake and gas was discovered. The well was Rabbit Lake No. 1 (originally named Running Rabbit Lake by Don Campbell).

Stan Harding sets out to study the McMurray Formation in beautiful northern Alberta. Photo provided by Sproule Associates.

Cam examines the Hay River Devonian reef outcrop, 1954.
Photo reproduced with permission of World Oil *magazine.*

In 1955, Charlie Bulmer stood in for geologist Lionel Singleton on a field party for Briggs in the same area. Stan was party chief. Charlie fondly remembered their wind-up party at the end of the summer. An "old-timer" in the area, who had been caretaker for equipment left at the campsite, supplied some over-proof rum (not yet available in Alberta but sold in the Territories). Charlie, being a youngster and never having experimented with over-proof rum before, drank more than his fair share, leaving him a little "hung over" the next day. He recalled that Stan, either to teach him a lesson or to take delight in what had happened, "sent me shimmying up a tall tree to recover the antenna for our radio—the last thing you want to do when you're under the weather!" (For the first time, the crew was equipped with a radio, and were able to stay in contact with Calgary while out in the bush.)

In those days, Sproule could boast that their clients were the only ones exploring north of the sixtieth parallel. As a result of Sproule's survey work in the Mackenzie River Basin, a total of 29 wells and 41 test holes were drilled between 1951 and 1956.

In 1957, Western Minerals, a Sproule client, drilled the first well within the Arctic Circle. Although the well was abandoned, a second well was drilled in 1959, encountering oil and gas. The previous year, Cam had said, "Without much doubt we are dealing with a rich oil basin." Western Minerals' success enhanced Sproule's reputation in the oil community.

Sproule field parties moved farther and farther north. In a letter to A.R. Coad of the Department of Northern Affairs, dated June 20, 1959, Cam summarized work Sproule undertook in the Lower Mackenzie Basin. Sproule was conducting detailed geological surveys for the Atlantic Refining Company, Texaco Canada Ltd., Shell Oil of Canada, Amerada Petroleum Corp., Dome Exploration, Dome Petroleum, and Charter Oil Company.

By this time, the field parties had increased in size, and usually included two senior geologists, two junior geologists, two helicopter crews, a cook, and a part-time Beaver airplane crew. Rubber dinghies and canoes continued to be used.

In 1959, while working at Norman Wells, Stan was impressed by the ease in which geological formations could be seen the farther north they went; unlike those in the south, they were not hidden by vegetation. The photogeology work was especially useful there. According to Stan, it was invaluable. In a letter to Cam from Fort Good Hope, N.W.T. in 1959, he wrote:

Photo-geological reconnaissance ahead of field reconnaissance ahead of section measuring really pays off in the efficiency of the total operation. A well selected section can be measured twice as fast and the results are twice as useful.

For Sproule, 1960 was a busy and highly successful year with respect to their northern operations: the company was directly involved in, or assisting, exploratory studies of more than 20 million acres in the Arctic Islands. After the Northwest Territories, the Arctic was a logical progression for Sproule; its barren landscapes were ideal for doing surface geology. Cam sent his first field parties into the Arctic in 1960. One of their field parties discovered a significant mineral deposit, a lead-zinc deposit, on Little Cornwallis Island. This led to the development of the Polaris Mine and excited Cam even more about the potential of Canada's North.

The massive field exploration programs in the Arctic Islands that went on through the 1960s affected the entire organization. A great deal of Sproule's work in the Islands was not funded, and cash in the company accounts was often lacking. Many employees remembered being asked to hold off cashing their pay cheques until funds became available.

Those in the Calgary office at that time (the engineers and subsurface geologists) worked hard to ensure that money flowed into the company, and to establish a reputation that set them apart as experts in the field of subsurface interpretations, reserve estimates, and evaluations. The company was committed to letting its clientele know that Sproule offered more than just exploration geology expertise and know-how, and a concerted effort was made to expand the subsurface geological and reservoir engineering evaluation sections.

Stan Harding studies iron springs in the Tathlina Lake area of the Northwest Territories. Photo provided by Sproule Associates.

The Bow Building

By mid-1959, the company had seen an influx of engineers, and more geologists had been hired for Arctic fieldwork. Sproule's office in the Baysel Building at Eighth Avenue and Eighth Street SW was old, run-down, and over-crowded. The employees were spread over three different locations in the downtown core, and time was being wasted running between them. It was time for Cam to find new office space.

Cam thought that the downtown core of Calgary would continue moving west, so he chose to construct his own building at the end of Fourth Avenue SW, adjacent to the Louise Bridge and the Bow River. The building, located at 1009 Fourth Avenue SW, would become known as the Bow Building. Cam, as usual, put all his energy into the planning and construction of the office. As a result, a beautiful, sturdy structure was built. In Oilweek *(June 1, 1970)*, Les Rowland wrote:

> It is composed of rough-cut stones, each of which is representative of some particular area and formation in Alberta, and is unique as a visual demonstration of regional geology.

"At the time, it was probably known as one of the most expensive buildings per square foot ever built in Calgary," said Earl Miller:

> Sproule imported teak from South America. The actual structure was only one floor with a raised type of basement. However, the foundation laid was sufficient to carry eight more floors, with a heliport on the roof.

Cam was determined to supply his own water to his new building on the Bow, believing that it would be an easy task, given the building's proximity to the river. He had a number of holes drilled in and around the building, hoping to tap into a water supply. Every hole came up dry. No doubt a bit disappointing for Cam

Cam's office building, unique at the time, faces the banks of Calgary's Bow River. Photo provided by the Sproule family.

the geologist! Finally, a ditch was dug by the river and water was piped into the building. The building was water-heated and -cooled, and this became a problem, said Charlie Bulmer, in Calgary's quickly changing weather:

> Turning the boiler on or off seemed to be a major operation, so it was turned on in the fall and off in the spring. A spell of unusual weather in the late fall or early spring made it very uncomfortable. You could dress for the cold, but I can remember days that your working papers would literally stick to your sweaty palms!

Wally Drew, one of Sproule's photogeologists, remembered that Cam always refused to call the basement the basement, *but insisted on calling it* the lower floor. *Of course the employees who worked on the lower floor always called it* the basement. *The company relocated to its new building on July 20, 1959.*

Putting it on Paper

Once Sproule field parties completed their survey work and returned to Calgary, the senior field geologists prepared the reports to the client. The reports covered all aspects of the clients' area, in particular, interpretation of the subsurface geology based on the field observations, analysis of potential reservoir rocks based on samples from outcrops, and discussion of potential prospects that could lead to oil or gas discoveries. Sketches of sections measured in the field, and preliminary maps prepared on site, were also fine-tuned and included in the final report.

Mickey Crockford apparently set the tone for good report writing. George Hunter, a geologist hired in 1959, recalled that Crockford (a former school teacher) was known as the "English Scholar." Charlie Bulmer remembered that Mickey initially revised everything he wrote. In retrospect, he thought it was worthwhile, because it made him take his time and produce a well written report.

The reports were originally typed with five carbon copies. In later years, one copy was typed on Ozalid paper and copies made by running them through the Ozalid machine; later, Xerox machines were used. Franky Cooper, a long-term Sproule secretary, cherished by all for her incomparable typing skills and work ethic, remembered doing typing for Cam:

The top brass put the finishing touches on a client's report. From left: Stan Harding, Cam, and Tony Edgington. Photo provided by the Sproule family.

> He was the sort of person who sailed into your office and slapped something down on your desk. And if you didn't hear what he said to you the first time, you *chased* him back to his office at the opposite corner of the building.

Often Cam presented his typists with wet cardboard inserts from his dry-cleaned shirts, the ink running from a letter or memo he had written while in the tub. Franky remembered that it was not just Dr. Sproule's typing that was always done in a rush—all of the work seemed to have a deadline. When the men came back with their data from the north, there was always a big rush to get the reports out to clients.

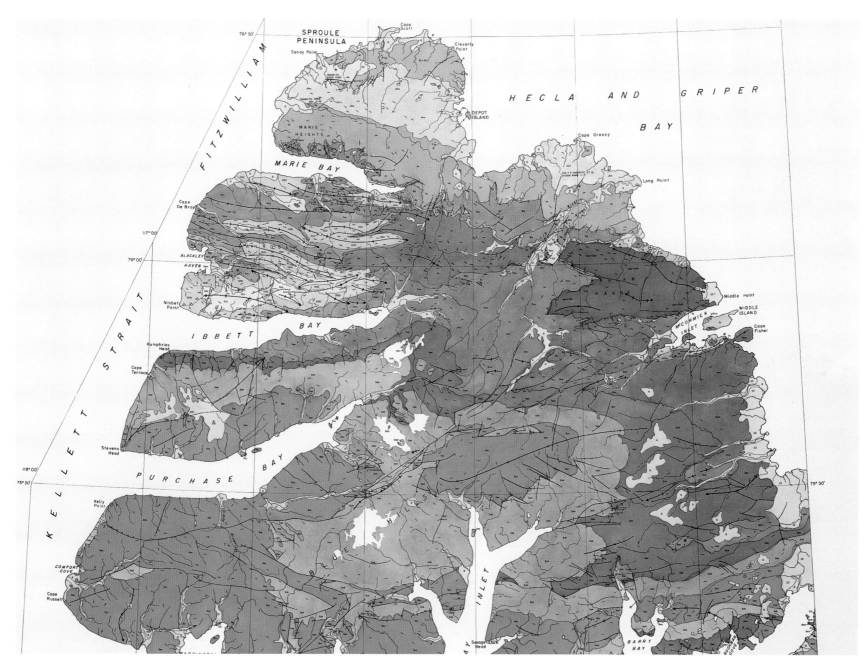

Melville Island.

Map Art

Cam realized early on that maps were essential for illustrating the geology of a certain area. One of the techniques Cam developed was to represent the outcrop pattern of each geological formation in a different colour on photomosaics or topographic maps of the Arctic Islands. Because each formation had to be individually coloured, the process of creating these maps was a time-consuming and painstaking procedure.

Initially, Cam coaxed Maude, Judy, and Anne into the office to colour maps. Anne remembered having to re-do their mother's because they were so bad. As the number of Sproule clients increased, Cam hired more and more women to do the colouring, resulting in a small army working in a room specifically dedicated to that purpose.

One of the numerous assistants that Zoltan Simon, one-time head of the colouring room, hired was Nora Tettensor. She explained how meticulous the colouring of the maps was.

At first, I was all by myself, but eventually we had 12 people. The hand work that we did was very, very time-consuming. We cut masks out of Mylar, a clear plastic—a different mask for every colour. We coloured the map by hand, using the Mylar masks like stencils, checking to make sure that every little piece had its colour. We did a map many, many times on linen, sort of an oil-cloth–type linen. They were a piece of artwork, really. We got so that we could do them very, very fast, but it was expensive.

Nora Tettensor (foreground) works diligently alongside other colouring room staff. Photo provided by Sproule Associates.

The colours were put on with our fingers, with tissues and cloths. We would dip it in the colour and then rub it on. We then had to rub it off so that it didn't streak—so that the colours were even. It was all done with the tip of your finger through the stencil, and you couldn't go over the edge, but if your stencil moved, you had to take your Exacto knife and scrape the little edges off so that the little blue lines would show. You had to be good with your hands. Everything was absolutely hand done.

Sometimes Dr. Sproule would come down, and I would haul a map out and roll it out on the floor. The client, he and I, and everybody else, would be crawling around on the floor.

Customers received only an original map; it was an original painting. There was no colour reproduction. My job afterward was to go over the map and see that everything was done, because things could be missed. Then we took it up to a room upstairs off drafting. It was not vented the way it should have been. We sprayed with an acrylic spray to preserve it.

I put in 16-hour days sometimes, because the maps had to be ready or the whole company would collapse.

Dora Bayerle, another colouring room employee, reported that in the 1960s there were up to 22 young ladies at a time doing hand colouring.

Cam was not all work and no play. He enjoyed, among other things, hunting, skating, and gardening, and he loved to play cards. He spent many hours playing gin rummy with good friend Gus Beck, and poker with U of A buddies Wally Smith and Grey Sharp.

But Cam took to his leisure activities with such energy that to some it looked more like work than relaxation. "We'd go hunting," recalled his friend Don Cooke, "and he'd see an area he liked, so he'd buy the whole quarter section. We all had dogs. Cam got a dog—then he had two dogs—then he was raising dogs!"

Cam became very attached to his dogs. When his dog Jube developed a spinal tumour, Judy said her father could not accept it. He sent the dog to the veterinary college in Guelph, Ontario, and then had his physician friend, John Noakes, examine him, all the while carrying Jube everywhere because he couldn't walk.

Cam was proud of his hunting prowess and his knowledge of wildlife. However, his so-called expertise on one occasion could not extricate him from the long arm of the law. In October 1961, Cam was forced to plead guilty under Section 19 of the Games Act to possession of a dead hen pheasant. At the time, he swore to the games officer that it belonged to a friend and that it was not a hen pheasant, it was a cock. He pursued this claim with his customary vigor, as can be seen from the impassioned letter he wrote to a Mr. Brunsden, Brooks, Alberta, October 26, 1961:

> *As explained, my case has to do with a charge that I was in possession of a hen pheasant. This bird happens to have been shot by one of my friends, but the responsibility for its presence in my car is mine. On the other hand, none of us believe it to be a hen pheasant because of its plumage, which was in part a rich brown in both tail and breast. The eye had red "turkey" mottling. It is not a typical young cock nor is it a typical hen. We considered well before keeping it. The Game officer claimed it was a hen but was apparently not qualified to examine it on the spot and prove the point. In any event, the bird has been sent to the University of Alberta for examination and the result will be available at a hearing in Magistrate Wade's office at 2 p.m. October 28.*

Cam paid a local lawyer $91 to handle the case and plead guilty, applying soon after to have his upland licence returned to him. One assumes the licence was duly reinstated.

Cam wanted every aspect of the exploratory work included in his clients' reports. He would, in his quest for perfection, drive his employees to distraction. Nora Tettensor, hired to colour maps, recalled:

> I don't think he ever designated authority to anyone. I don't think he ever truly trusted anybody. He just wanted it to be absolutely perfect when it went out of his office. I think he felt if something got out that was less than perfect, then he took the blame for it.

Not only would Cam demand perfect reports, he always seemed to work his staff into a frenzy in order to meet what some felt were artificial deadlines. More than one employee of Cam's said that he was determined to keep his staff working Friday afternoons. Never one to tolerate laziness or an inadequate effort, he would make sure no-one was "slacking off." "By Friday afternoon," Rein de Wit recalled, "Cam's mouth was twitching. He was tense and completely worked up to finalize some jobs that had to go out that afternoon." If Cam didn't like how a report looked, it was done again until it met with his approval. George Hunter fondly recalled Cam leaping into a room like Groucho Marx. "He grabbed the two sides of the table to look at a report, and the only thing missing was a cigar!"

Weekends were no different. Often the office was filled with people working—from typists to geologists to draftsmen. Engineer Hans Garde-Hansen remembered Cam arriving at his house one Saturday morning. Hans was gardening and Cam said, "I have to get something out by Monday. I can't do it. I need you to go and do it." Cam then offered to do the gardening if Hans would go down to the office. Hans returned later that day to find his yard work completed by his boss. Henri Wennekers also remembered working late at night and on Saturdays. Henri said he would never forget Cam coming in to the office:

He used to have shoes with rubber soles, and he would come walking through the hallways and you'd hear *swivel, swavel, swivel, swavel*. He stopped once and asked me, "What are you doing here?" I said, "Well, I'm working." "Good," he replied, and he'd go back down the hall, *swivel, swavel, swivel, swavel*.

As the 1960s wore on, Cam directed more and more of his energy to getting funding for Panarctic Oils, his "dream" company that would ultimately represent a consortium of Arctic Islands permit holders. Meanwhile, the engineering and subsurface geological departments began to get some sizeable jobs, and there was plenty of work to go around. The company had three main departments: engineering, subsurface geology, and surface geology, headed by Tony Edgington, Al Gorrell, and Gordon Jones, respectively. There were two engineering groups—petroleum engineering and gas engineering—the division having occurred naturally when John Maughan and Gus Van Wielingen joined Sproule. The drafting department, still under Gordon McCracken, also played a large part in expediting field parties to the North.

By the end of the decade, work began to run out for Sproule's largest department—the surface department—and they began to show substantial losses. The company made an effort to get into surface geological work overseas, in countries such as Iran, Algeria, Yemen, India, and Kuwait, and although some work was done internationally, operational problems to a large extent made the effort less worthwhile than first thought. International work continued, nevertheless, and in the 1990s, foreign countries became ripe for Sproule's evaluation work. A separate division of Sproule—Sproule International Limited—was incorporated in 1994.

Fun with the Boss

Anne Zoumer, who joined Sproule's accounting department in 1963 (a position she still holds today), remembered that Stampede time always included a trip for the employees to the Petroleum Club. Everyone, including Cam in his Panama hat, would walk from the Louise Bridge to the Club, have a few drinks (though Cam, himself, did not drink—no more than a beer before dinner) and a few dances, and head back to the office. "It was very civilized," said Anne, compared perhaps to today's Stampede lunches, which often carry on into the wee hours of the following morning.

Cam readies his camera at a Sproule picnic, 1958.
Photo provided by Jean Gorrell.

Another favourite was the company barbecue. Al Gorrell did the cooking, and Cam insisted the coffee be boiled three times, camp-style. Anne recalled the year the event was held near Turner Valley. Some of the employees were playing volleyball with Cam and Anne's husband, Rudi. Anne thought her career at Sproule was over when Rudi served a rather wet and muddy ball that connected with Cam's face. But her boss, who always had a sense of humour, laughed it off and all was forgotten.

At Christmas, a big lunch for the employees was held in the drafting room of the Bow Building. Again, Al did the cooking and Cam sliced and passed out the turkey, slipping any less-than-perfect slices to the employees' children and his own grandchildren. Santa always made an appearance to a receptive crowd and passed out gifts supplied by Maude Sproule.

Colin Risk, senior reservoir technician, remembered one Christmas three or four of the engineers gathered in one of the offices to have a drink:

We were all sitting there when Dr. Sproule came in the office and we thought, "Well, this is the end." He started laughing and talking to us, and he had a drink himself. We got talking about this and that, and the next thing you know he was on the desk doing a one-arm handstand.

Corporate Politics

Almost from the beginning, Sproule employees grumbled about the lack of raises and Cam's hesitance to share ownership of the consultancy. It wasn't until 1969, after much "discussion" between Cam and his key people, that he would relent and agree to distribute 49 percent of the shares of the company to his associates (although the full 49 percent were not distributed right away). "Up to that time," Keith Williams said, "we all worked on the strength of the future."

Keith said Cam was more interested in geology than in matters pertaining to personnel. His lack of attention to raises, for example, was not because he was miserly, but because he simply did not think about it. This attitude however, caused conflict and bitterness between Cam and some of his employees; Sproule lost some top-notch people to high-paying companies. Others gained excellent experience at Sproule and then ventured out on their own. "It was common knowledge," said Anne Zoumer, "that some geologists worked for Sproule simply to be able to put 'Sproule' on their résumé." Those who stayed were stimulated by the work at Sproule, stuck it out, and fought to persuade Cam that his Associates deserved more than he was offering.

Cam's daughters said their father was not interested in money and never went after money for money's sake. Anne said that he often felt betrayed when people left him to go after more lucrative positions. He just could not understand it: he believed people should want to work for him because the work was so satisfying—wages should not factor into the equation. Indeed, in Earl Miller's recollection, Cam never took a salary or draw while he was head of Sproule.

Cam initially considered distributing shares in his company in 1954, when he first incorporated J.C. Sproule and Associates Limited. However, no progress was made in this regard within the organization, and on March 15, 1957, the company was struck from the Register.

The company was again incorporated in 1960 as J.C. Sproule and Associates Ltd., with two incorporation shares held by members of the MacKimmie Matthews law firm—Gordon Allen and his secretary Myrtle Egleston. The annual report for the year ending December 31, 1961 still showed Cam holding 60,000 of the ordinary shares and all 30,000 of the issued preference shares. Gordon Allen still held one nominal share and had been appointed a director in June 1961. His secretary had relinquished her share that same month, and it was transferred to Harold Barclay of Price Waterhouse. The officers appointed in June 1961 included Cam Sproule, president and general manager; Gordon Allen, vice-president; and Willa Tegart, secretary-treasurer.

Cam Lends a Hand

One day, Al Gorrell was looking for help to move a table from his office to another location. A member of the staff walked by and Al asked him if he could lend a hand, to which the person replied, "That's not what I was hired for."

Moments later, Cam strode by and asked Al what he was doing. Al said, "I want to move this table." Cam immediately grabbed one end of the table and the two men moved it down the hall. On the way, they passed the employee who had refused to help, and Al said to him, nodding towards Cam, "So what was he hired for!"

It was not until October 1962 that a permanent structure was put in place. The meeting setting up the new arrangement took place October 17, 1962. The Board of Directors of the company consisted of Cam, Stan Harding (Sproule's executive vice-president), John Maughan, and Gus Van Wielingen. Rein de Wit and Mickey Crockford replaced Gordon Allen and Harold Barclay, who resigned as Directors. Some senior professional employees were named Associates: Clark Smith, Charlie Bulmer, Tony Edgington, Gordon Jones, Don Campbell, and Al Gorrell. Neither the Directors nor the Associates had any financial interest in the company; this continued for almost a decade. (At the time of the incorporation, Cam did give each of his Directors and Associates a cheque, as a token of his appreciation.) The Directors of Sproule became an "Executive Committee," instituted to plan and run the consulting business, according to Charlie—"a 'de facto' Board of Directors without share representation." Stan Harding received one share in September 1964, transferred to him by Barclay, and Gordon Allen held his nominal share until the final distribution in 1969.

Probably because Cam did not make his executive staff part owners of the company, a corporate crisis arose early in 1961. Harold Barclay and Gordon Allen had been asked to prepare a profit-sharing plan, which they completed on January 25, 1961. A short time later some of the Directors met with accounting firm Peat Marwick on the subject of share distribution in J.C. Sproule and Associates.

The letter prepared for the directors by Gordon Burton of Peat Marwick, and copied to Cam, describes how, as a sole proprietorship, the income for each year fluctuated significantly: in 1957 it was $27,000, whereas in 1958 it was $127,000. It also pointed out that upon Cam's death, unless a plan of succession was in place, the value of the firm could virtually disappear. Goodwill of $300,000 was attributed to the company by Peat Marwick, of which $84,000 Dr. Sproule had attributed to his associates. Peat Marwick suggested that 49 percent of the company be sold to its Associates, in a reasonable and timely fashion. It was further suggested that if someone were to leave the company, his or her shares could be bought out pro rata by the remaining shareholders.

Cam was less than impressed. His letter to Allen and Barclay three days later was scathing and at times vitriolic, taking the position that he was under no obligation to make a deal with his Associates, that all the risks and work done to date were his alone, and that they had all been paid adequately for their work:

Sproule "Bean Counter"

When I became treasurer of Sproule, Cam's introduction of me to clients and business associates invariably included the following story. When he left to go to South America, there were five floors of productive geologists and engineers and one floor of accounting clerks in International's six-story Toronto office building. When he returned some four years later, there was only one floor of productive staff and five floors of accounting clerks. "I have warned Earl that the accountants are not going to breed like rabbits in my company," he would say—and we didn't.

Earl Miller

This whole proposal is so ridiculous that I would feel inclined to suggest to my Associates that if they really think they can run a business of this sort they should do so on their own. If they believe they can, why divide the fruits of their labours with me? On the other hand I am not sure that all of them are behind this suggestion. I think they are all a bit stunned by Burton's proposal.

Cam felt that Gus Van Wielingen and John Maughan, more than the others, were unhappy with the deal offered them. John left the company in 1964 to enter into the oil company management business. (Tony replaced him as chief engineer.) Any hard feelings that may have existed were put aside, however, as evidenced by Cam's letter to John at the time of his departure: "We will be pleased to work with you on any mutually agreeable basis that may appear to be to the benefit of both parties." Mickey Crockford and Gus Van Wielingen resigned as Directors in 1964, and Rein de Wit resigned as a Director in June 1965. Cam and Gus also parted on good terms, and Gus started his own company, called Sulpetro. Gus said years later that, despite the problems Cam had with the concept of his Associates participating in the firm, on a personal basis it couldn't have been any better between them. "He never treated me just as an employee—he treated me as a friend."

On July 24, 1965, an executive meeting was held for the Directors. It was a Saturday; Cam did not believe in wasting company time on such administrative necessities as staff meetings. In attendance were Charlie Bulmer, Tony Edgington, Al Gorrell, Stan Harding, and Gordon Jones. (Charlie and Gordon had just been made Directors in June.) The issue was again raised regarding Directors' participation in the company. Cam spoke about the frustrations in the past of trying to find a workable formula for participation, but agreed that it was necessary in principle and that something should be done. Tony urged that the matter be dealt with at an early date, and suggested a staff meeting to review the issue. Again, nothing was resolved.

Finally, in 1969, after much persistence on the part of the Directors (in particular Tony Edgington), Cam distributed shares to all his senior employees based on a shareholders' agreement signed by all the parties. Under the agreement, 49 percent of all the shares could eventually be distributed, allowing Cam to maintain control. Noel Cleland, past president of Sproule, remarked: "Cam finally had sufficient confidence in the people working for him that he let them have a small piece of the business." Even then, the full 49 percent was not distributed.

Cam, Charlie Bulmer, Don Campbell, Noel Cleland, Tony Edgington, Al Gorrell, and Stan Harding were on the Board of Directors. Stan was vice-president; Tony, executive vice-president;

Charlie, head of subsurface geology; Don, head of surface geology and photogeology; Noel, head of natural gas engineering; and Al, head of industrial minerals and special projects. Each Director had share participation, as did Gordon Allen and Sproule Associates Geoff Alderman, Doug Bietz, Mike Brusset, Jim Chilton, John Stuart-Smith, and Jim Terrill. In addition to Cam's shares (60,000), a total of 27,477 of the 100,000 authorized no par value shares were held. Cam alone held 23,890 of the 30,000 preference shares. He personally decided who would be shareholders and what their participation would be.

Accomplishments Along the Way

Cam had joined various organizations as soon as he moved back to Calgary from Toronto. He was never at a loss for energy: not only did he run a flourishing consultancy and author various papers on geological subjects, he also sought out senior positions in the Association of Professional Engineers of Alberta (APEA) (later known as the Association of Professional Engineers, Geologists, and Geophysicists of Alberta (APEGGA)), the Canadian Institute of Mining and Metallurgy (CIM), and the American Association of Petroleum Geologists (AAPG). Besides providing intellectual stimulation and comradery, both very important to Cam, he could meet people and market the work of his consultancy.

Cam's objective as president of the APEA for the 1957-58 term was to convince APEA engineers to include geologists and geophysicists in their organization. Prior to 1960, all professionals in the oil business had the P.Eng. designation, regardless of their particular specialty. Cam reached his objective: geologists and geophysicists were allowed to join the APEA, and two new designations were established—P.Geol. and P.Geoph. "Cam Sproule was a major player in the changeover," said Alex Hemstock, former president of the APEA. "It was a pioneer effort, because no other association in Canada had any pressure on them to include geologists. Cam made the case very well and very strongly."

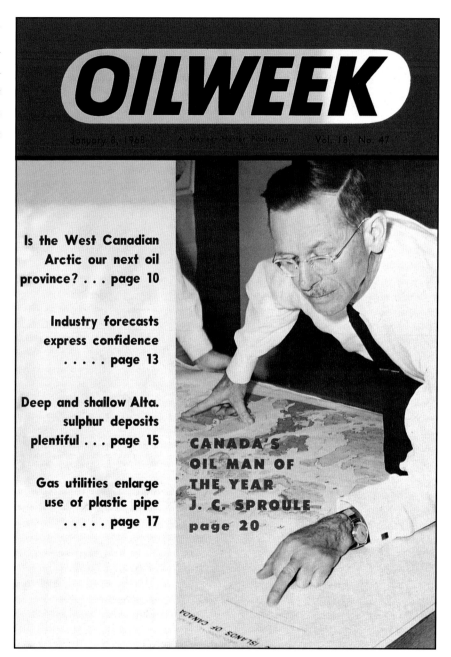

OILWEEK

January 8, 1968   A Maclean-Hunter Publication   Vol. 18, No. 47

Is the West Canadian Arctic our next oil province? . . . page 10

Industry forecasts express confidence . . . . . page 13

Deep and shallow Alta. sulphur deposits plentiful . . . page 15

Gas utilities enlarge use of plastic pipe . . . . . page 17

CANADA'S OIL MAN OF THE YEAR J. C. SPROULE page 20

Cam becomes Oilweek's *Man of the Year, 1968. Cover reproduced with permission of* Oilweek *magazine.*

Cam Takes on the CPR

The year 1963 was a hectic one for Cam and his company. As Charlie Bulmer recalled, anything Cam was involved in, the whole office got into. Not only was Cam elected president of the AAPG that year, he became involved in a lengthy debate with the City of Calgary over the Canadian Pacific Railway's proposal to divert the railway tracks from Ninth Avenue in downtown Calgary to land adjacent to the south shore of the Bow River. The CPR's plan was to put office buildings along Ninth Avenue and run the tracks parallel to the Bow River. Cam opposed the plan vehemently: he felt the tracks along the riverfront would forever spoil the area for Calgarians, and the Bow Building would be destroyed—the plan called for a 200-foot right-of-way, and the corner of the building was only 117 feet from the river's edge. (This latter concern was less important, because Cam could have made a substantial amount of money had he sold his property to the City.)

Cam was incensed that some of the City aldermen supported the CPR's proposal without a proper study of the advantages and disadvantages of the plan. (Jack Leslie, alderman and elected mayor of Calgary in 1965, was ardently opposed to the plan.) Property tax implications, city planning, and financing were all issues Cam and other citizens felt were being ignored.

The project, initiated by Rod Sykes of Marathon Realty (Sykes became mayor of Calgary in 1969), was threatened by lawsuits on the part of a large number of property owners south of the Bow River, who feared the new right-of-way would significantly devalue their property. The property owners urged the City, and later the provincial legislature, to halt the proposed development until a proper engineering study was completed. They wanted to know the feasibility of depressing the tracks or moving them outside Calgary. Another concern was that the CPR would be granted a tax exemption by the City, placing them in a privileged position compared to other Calgary taxpayers.

Cam immediately went to work on local service clubs, getting his word out to as many Calgarians as possible. The first of his speeches was made at the Canadian Club on May 23, 1963. He talked about the tax issue (current CPR property was not taxed), and reminded his audience of the irreplaceable scenic value of the Bow River:

> No study of the overall economic impact of the whole project on the City of Calgary has yet been made by experts on the staff of the City or by consultants acting for the City. The problem is obviously a complicated one and should not be finally decided on the whim of uninformed City employees. City Council must insist on such outside advice before passing on the proposal. If

they do not, the day that any overall proposal passes, involving use of the river bank for the C.P.R. trackage, could be one of the blackest in the history of the city of Calgary.

On September 30, 1963, Cam appeared before the Glendale Kiwanis Club:

> I was impressed by the preliminary preparations made by City Planners to improve the aesthetic value of the downtown river front acreage, so I purchased several lots near the Louise Bridge and made plans, with the approval of the City, to build an office building.... I have a right, as do all of you, to know the long-term economic effect on the City of Calgary of the proposal to re-locate the railway tracks along the river bank.

On February 12, 1964 at the Victoria School, Cam spoke to the Alberta Old Age Pensioners Society, where he said he would withdraw his objections to the plan if the City agreed to an independent study of the proposal. He knew he was being referred to as a man with an axe to grind, "because of the location of my office building along the proposed right-of-way," but responded:

> Of course I have an axe to grind as does every taxpayer in the City of Calgary. For my part, I think I cleaned my hands of any dirty implications when I agreed to cease opposing the scheme if a comprehensive study were made.

Cam leaves the podium satisfied he's said his piece.
Photo provided by Glenbow Archives, Calgary.

Three independent studies were made, none of them conclusive. Sproule wound up saying, "The City Council and the taxpayers will be entirely defenceless without some knowledge of the long-term taxation and other effects on the City of Calgary."

Ultimately, the Alberta government received a request from the City of Calgary to pass legislation on the project. Briefs were submitted to then Premier Ernest Manning. The CPR matter was scheduled to be heard on March 2, 1964 by the entire Legislature. Representatives of the City, the CPR, and Calgarians for Progress (in favour of the relocation), presented their views. The Calgary Chamber of Commerce and lawyers for the South Bow Bank Property Association also submitted briefs.

The hearing lasted over a period of three days and, according to The Albertan *(March 5, 1964):*

> The crucial moment came when Premier Manning and C.P.R. Vice-President Ian Sinclair agreed across the floor of the House on two clauses to be written into the City-C.P.R. contract to clear the way for enabling legislation…. One of the clauses is to add in provincial expropriation rights. The other is to free the province from C.P.R.'s tax free status if there is a federal change.

Wrangling continued for months over the enabling legislation. City aldermen and Calgary citizens continued to battle over the hotly contested scheme. Ultimately, Jack Leslie, Cam Sproule, and all those against the plan triumphed: Calgary's city council voted the plan down, and the proposed re-location of Calgary's train tracks was put to rest.

Cam had dealt with the press many times, and was mentioned often in the Calgary Herald *during the CPR fight.* Oilweek's *Les Rowland (June 1, 1970) commented:*

> For the press he was a sheer delight to interview, courteous and never impatient with the interviewer, although sometimes with himself. His opinions were incisive and he seldom asked for anything he said to be kept "off the record."

During Cam's struggle with the CPR, his friend Ted Link held a birthday party for himself, as he always did. Don Cooke remembered one of Cam's friends, Don McKenzie, mounting a toy train on a board and presenting it to Cam, together with an engineer's hat emblazoned with "CPR." "Cam thought it was wonderful."

APEGGA honoured Cam ten years later, at their Annual Meeting on March 29, 1968. Cam was presented with the Centennial Award, bestowed on a member

who has attained unusual distinction in the arts relating to the sciences of engineering, geology or geophysics in the teaching of major courses in these fields; or who by reason of invention, research, original work, or as an executive on projects of unusual important scope, has made substantial contributions to the foregoing fields; and who has attained the age of 40 years and has been in good standing as a member of the Association for a period of at least five years prior to the date of his nomination for the award.

The year 1959 saw Cam become president of the CIM. He had joined the organization in 1951, and encouraged his employees to join. In 1954, Cam was appointed Chairman of the Petroleum and Natural Gas (P&NG) division, and in this capacity lobbied for the creation of a technical library relating to petroleum and natural gas. The library was established in 1955.

Cam's main objectives while president of the Montreal-based CIM were to set up an office in Western Canada and to establish a Western-based quarterly publication for petroleum and natural gas papers. Cam felt, and reasonably so, that the office in Montreal could not adequately address the needs and services of its Western members. He suggested that a Western office would encourage more professionals to join the organization's P&NG division instead of joining competing organizations. In the late 1950s and early 1960s, capital investment in the Canadian oil industry had been greater than in all other mining and resource industries in the country, and Cam felt the provinces responsible for encouraging that investment deserved the financial support of the CIM.

In October 1961, the Executive Council of the CIM made available an amount not exceeding $25,000 to appoint a field secretary for Western Canada. The field secretary's job was to develop membership in the P&NG division, and to organize a quarterly publication. John Ditchburn, an engineer with a background in law and editing, was hired. The inaugural issue of the *Journal of Canadian Petroleum Technology* (JCPT) contained seven technical papers. Despite Ditchburn's excellent credentials and Cam's efforts to see the Western office and its publication a success, the endeavour ultimately failed. The office closed and Ditchburn moved on to other opportunities.

Cam would, even after his presidency, try to convince the CIM to move its headquarters from Montreal to Toronto, no doubt to make the organization appear more national in its outlook. Dick Barrett, executive director in 1964, agreed with Cam but felt the mining interests in Quebec would

---

Doctor's Orders

According to Judy Sproule, Cam's passion for all that he did was not without consequence. In 1954, his physician told him if he didn't take a holiday, he'd be dead in a year. Cam took the doctor's advice, no doubt with great urging from Maude. However, even on vacation Cam could not sit still. Maude wrote her daughters from Florida saying that he was up at five each morning, helping the locals clean the beach.

vehemently oppose it. He also thought some people associated with companies operating in Quebec would fear retaliation by the Quebec government if the CIM moved its offices: "Duplessis [*past premier of Quebec*] left a very deep mark on the people in Quebec and the local scene is not entirely free of fear even today." The CIM headquarters is still in Montreal.

In 1972, two years after Cam's death, the CIM established The John Campbell Sproule Memorial Plaque on the recommendation of many members of the Petroleum Society of the CIM. In its August 1972 *Bulletin*, it stated:

> The late Dr. J.C. Sproule made an outstanding impression on the Institute, the industry and every-one he came in contact with during his long and varied career.

> The plaque was established

> to perpetuate the memory of, and to give recognition to, the man who, through his visionary zeal and professional dedication, contributed so greatly to the early widespread appreciation of Canada's Arctic resource potential.

Ted Link, Cam's boss in the early days at Imperial Oil, was the first recipient of the award (April 23, 1974).

In 1963, J.C. Sproule and Associates operated largely without Cam's daily presence. (For some, it made getting the job done a little easier, and it was a lot less stressful!) Cam was away most of the year after being elected the 47th president of the American Association of Petroleum Geologists (AAPG)—a feat no other Canadian before him had accomplished. Cam's Campaign Manager was Ted Link, and his election committee sent out letters encouraging all Americans who knew Cam to write to their colleagues about him. Cam had also campaigned on his own behalf, making five separate trips to the United States to make himself known to geologists.

At an AAPG luncheon meeting held on October 29, 1962, Cam thanked Ted and other friends who assisted him in his campaign: "I appreciate what my friends are doing. Help offered, even by competing consultants, is something I won't be able to forget in a hurry."

> Bill Gallup and John Andrichuk and Ralph Edie also came to me and offered to write letters in support of my candidacy. I sure would hate to fall down on that kind of support, not to mention all the others who are putting a great deal of time and effort into the project. I don't deserve all the help that I'm getting, but I'll take it. That may be the Scotch in me. They say of a Scotsman, as a

J. C. Sproule Memorial Wildlife Research Foundation

For some years prior to his death, Cam owned a quarter section of land in the Rolling Hills area of Alberta, the area where he did most of his hunting. The only improvement on the land was an old building he had fixed up as a hunting lodge. According to Cam's hunting buddies, the "lodge" was really no more than a shack, but it suited their purpose and was fondly remembered by all who spent time there.

Photo provided by Lorne Fitch.

In a letter to Maude after Cam's death, dated July 22, 1970, the operations manager for the Alberta Wildlife Foundation, W.R. Morgan, wrote that Cam had discussed the Rolling Hills land with him prior to his death, expressing big conservation plans for the area:

> *His project at Rolling Hills was one of his greatest ambitions and he was so enthusiastic on what had been accomplished and how he hoped to expand the operations to include three more quarters of land. He had made such headway with the farmers in the vicinity in bringing his thoughts on wildlife to them.*

> *In this day and age of wanton destruction, it is a shame to lose such a dedicated conservationist.*

After Cam died, his family sold the land to Ted Link, Don Cooke, Doug Leitch, and Wilf Loucks, Cam's hunting companions. Because of the lack of bird habitat and deteriorating conditions, they decided to restore it, and the J.C. Sproule Memorial Wildlife Research Foundation was established. The group contacted Ducks Unlimited, who agreed to create a set of ponds and sloughs in order to lure wildlife to the area. (Their other idea—setting up a game reserve— was turned down by the government.) The provincial government ultimately bought the land but was required to honour the lease to Ducks Unlimited in perpetuity. It is now, according to Don Cooke, a tract of land that Cam would have been proud of, with white-tailed deer, pheasants, and lush vegetation providing shelter for all the birds of the area.

measure of his capacity on a drinking spree, that he can drink any given quantity. That is about the way I feel about the manner of my candidacy as I realize that my opponent is going to provide pretty tough opposition.

Once elected, Cam commented that his election was

> a fine commentary on the operations of democratic principles as between two neighbouring countries. Eleven thousand or more of the thirteen thousand voting members are U.S. citizens, yet they elected a foreigner. That sort of thing could not have occurred anywhere outside North America, even among professional men.

Cam's main objective as AAPG President was to obtain certification of qualified members of the AAPG as professional petroleum geologists. He felt the public image of the geologist was deficient, and if the AAPG certified them, it would help improve their standing. To him, a geologist was a scientist and thus a professional, and should be designated as one. He felt it would be a major benefit to the public and to the profession itself to have certification. Further, in order to ensure that the best public image was conveyed, he felt a uniform code of ethics should be established, so members could be disciplined when they fell below a set standard. Certification, therefore, meant meeting specific standards in professional education and experience, as well as strict adherence to a professional code of ethics.

Unfortunately, Cam's hard work on this issue bore no fruit. Some members did not want it, others were desperate for it. In the end, the AAPG executive committee recommended certification on a purely voluntary basis. Cam urged all geologists on his staff to be certified.

Highlights of Cam's year-long presidency were his Chairmanship of the Petroleum Statistics and Education session of the Sixth World Petroleum Congress held in Frankfurt, West Germany, and the 1964 Annual Meeting held in Toronto, the first Annual Meeting held outside the United States.

Cam's contributions to his industry, and recognition for his work, continued. In 1967, he was one of the key influences in establishing the Institute of Sedimentary and Petroleum Geology in Calgary. The formation of the Institute created a major geological presence in Western Canada. He was also recognized by the Engineering Institute of Canada at their Annual Meeting in Montreal on May 31 of that same year, and presented with the Julian C. Smith medal for 1966. The medal, founded in 1939, was bestowed on Cam for his achievement in the development of Canada. Cam's daughters telegrammed him on the date of his investiture: "Congratulations, we're just busting with pride. Anne and Judy."

Finally, in 1968, *Oilweek* named Cam "Man of the Year." Editor Earle Gray, in the January 8 issue, described him as one of those people upon whom the future of Canada depends:

> The oil industry was built by men like Sproule, men with big ideas and the courage to back those ideas. Some have succeeded, many more have failed. Whether or not Sproule ultimately succeeds is not the important thing. The important thing is that there are men with vital ideas who are bold enough to back them to the hilt. It is on men like these that the future of Canada depends.

WILDERNESS TO WILDCAT

CONQUERING THE CANADIAN ARCTIC

It is high time that the popular image of the Arctic Archipelago
as a useless patch of snow and ice be dispelled.

Cam Sproule

Arctic hoodoos blaze orange in the midnight sun, Ellef Ringnes Island.
Photo provided by Sproule Associates.

53

Why the Arctic?

Cam Sproule called it the largest known undeveloped oil and gas basin in the Western Hemisphere. But for him, the potential of the Canadian Arctic was not limited to commercial resources: he saw the average Canadian family living there by the middle of the 21st century. "The myriads of lakes and streams which dot this area could develop into the personal properties and playgrounds of our citizens," he said in a presentation to the Pacific Northwest Trade Association in 1967. "Private airports and private aircraft flown by private citizens will probably have become routine." He even saw road and rail there in the future. He predicted that agriculture would be possible, and he did not see climatic conditions as a serious problem. He described the Arctic as a rough and unfriendly area in winter, but not in summer, and he felt that if need be, it could certainly be made more habitable. "Even today, space heating and the added comfort provided by suitable clothing can solve most climatic problems as applied to personal living conditions, even in the Arctic."

Up to 1948, regional geological maps contained little additional information about the Arctic Islands to that shown on Samuel Haughton's almost 100-year-old map. His was the first geological map of the Islands, a broad interpretation of information brought back by expeditions led by Captains Belcher, Kellett, Collinson, and M'Clure. A new era of Arctic Island exploration began when a small number of weather stations was established and the Geological Survey of Canada (GSC) started an extensive preliminary survey program. The airstrips at the weather stations allowed exploration during the short summer season using small aircraft such as the Piper Cub, Courier, Beaver, and Otter. The customary multi-year ship-borne expeditions posed considerable risk to both ship and explorer. The GSC surveys were of a regional nature; the basic geological framework of the sedimentary basins—the general stratigraphy and the structural trends—were examined, and some widely separate areas were mapped in detail. The GSC expeditions were

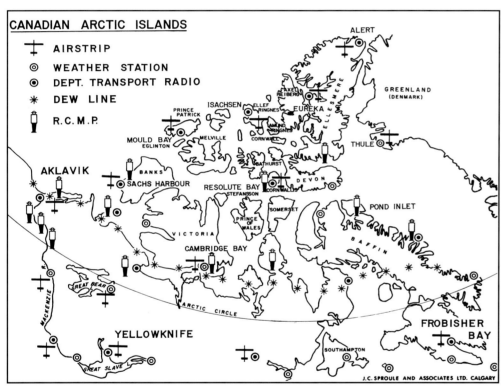

Sproule's map from the 1960s.

54

especially important because they showed promise for exploration geology in the Islands, and they demonstrated that summer exploration was possible. In 1955, the GSC undertook a major expedition, called Operation Franklin, which brought new insight into the regional geology.

In 1957, a GSC party successfully mapped the geology of portions of the Arctic Islands with the support of a small, fixed-wing aircraft equipped with oversize, low-pressure tires. These tires allowed aircraft to land safely on unprepared sites. Weldy Phipps, of Bradley Air Services, contributed greatly to their technical development, and was the first Arctic pilot to use them in the Islands.

GSC expeditions, and other smaller expeditions by private groups, paved the way for Cam Sproule and his company of exploration geologists. In a paper published in *The Canadian Mining and Metallurgical Bulletin* (December 1964), Cam and Rein de Wit, wrote: "It was particularly the preliminary results of the Survey expeditions that brought the Archipelago into the spotlight as a major potential oil and gas producing area." Sproule made extensive use of published GSC reports as a starting point for their exploration programs.

Also in the late 1950s, wartime and early post-war aerial photographs were made available by the federal government. Because of the general lack of vegetation, the rock formations in the Arctic Islands were exposed and could be interpreted from the photos. The photos revealed the presence of varied, thick sedimentary basins of many ages, from Precambrian (more than 570 million years old) to geologically recent times. Further, the Islands were in a region where geological structures had been formed by faulting and folding of the earth's crust, a process generally known to lead to the collection and trapping of oil and gas.

The Arctic Islands Sedimentary Basin is a northeastern extension of the Western Canadian Sedimentary Basin. Within the Islands it has a length along its northeastern axis of over 1,000 miles and a width from northwest to southwest of over 500 miles. From observations recorded in the Islands, Cam believed that the sedimentary section—as much as 60,000 feet thick in the deeper Sverdrup Basin—was similar to what was seen in oil and gas field areas of the interior of North America from the Gulf of Mexico to the lower Mackenzie Basin. The same animal and plant life responsible for the generation of oil in the known fields was also present in the geological formations of the Islands. For Cam, the Islands were probably as rich in oil and gas and in metallic and non-metallic minerals as were regions in southern Canada. In the 1964 *Bulletin* paper, Cam and Rein wrote:

Operation Franklin

Yves Fortier drew up plans for the 1955 Operation Franklin in response to demands made to the GSC by the Department of Northern Affairs, which was conscious of the potential development of the Arctic through previous GSC work. According to geologist Oscar Erdman, also with the GSC, Fortier had been given secret orders to look into the Arctic situation; at the time, sovereignty over the area was in question, and some feared the Russians coming "over the top." When he went to visit Fortier one night, he found him with maps of the Arctic scattered over the floor.

The objectives of Operation Franklin were to add to geological knowledge and to show Canadian activity in its own Arctic. A third objective—to investigate the potential for petroleum resources—emerged as knowledge of the sedimentary basin unfolded. Fortier was assisted by a number of people in preparing for and implementing the Operation, not the least of which was Ray Thorsteinsson (a graduate student in geology when introduced to Arctic exploration in 1950), who had a long and illustrious career with the GSC. Each senior member of the Operation was assisted by a post-graduate student, and they investigated a number of localities. The expeditions were supported by helicopter, and provided equipment and supplies for a period from one to four weeks; the work extended over some 200,000 square miles.

The total area and the total volume of prospective strata in the Arctic Islands are of the same magnitude as the sedimentary basin areas of Alberta, Saskatchewan and Manitoba put together. An imaginary composite section of formations in the Archipelago yields a stratigraphic column with a thickness of about ten miles, or twice the composite section of the Prairie Provinces.

Surface evidence of oil was abundant, including seepages, and the structures that could be expected to yield oil and gas were evident—structures already well known for the Western Canadian Sedimentary Basin. Almost all the usual stratigraphic, structural, and fault traps for oil and gas occurred on the Islands. Thick rock units with good porosity and permeability existed, as did probable source beds for oil and gas. "The geological setting is as ideal as one could expect," Cam said in an article published in *Oilweek* (January 16, 1960). In the *Bulletin* paper, he and Rein wrote: "Present geological information indicates that the Canadian Arctic Islands form a potential new oil and gas province, and further exploration is fully warranted."

Getting Started

It was inevitable that Cam Sproule enter the Arctic. The general lack of vegetation and the presence of substantial outcrops meant that the geology was exposed; for surface geologists like Cam, it was paradise. "The islands provide the most perfect field laboratory in the western hemisphere for studies of regional and local structure, facies and other stratigraphic data," he said in *Oilweek* (May 21, 1962). "Outside of mountain areas, I doubt that any other place on earth has a basin that provides equal prospects for facilitation of geological study."

A glacial lake forms north of Otto Fiord, Ellesmere Island. Photo provided by Walter Kupsch.

In addition, Sproule had spent the previous seven field seasons in the Northwest Territories, in conditions not unlike those of the Islands. Petroleum exploration had spread into the Territories between 1950 and 1955, and the company had undertaken much of the required geologic mapping of permits, developing special techniques necessary for examining large areas during the short northern summers, including the use of helicopters. They were accustomed to working a great distance from normal sources of supply, under harsh environmental conditions, and when the Arctic Islands play opened in 1958, Sproule was well prepared to undertake mapping assignments there.

In January 1959, the Government of Canada was surprised when several Canadian entrepreneurs, including Dan Bateman of Domex (Dominion Explorers), Bill Patterson of Trans-Western Oil, Bryce Cameron of Round Valley Oil, and Cam Sproule (who was acting on behalf of a number of clients), applied for exploratory permits. The Canadian government did not have appropriate regulations in place, but because it had an interest in resource development in Canada's northern frontier, it allowed the applicants to designate areas for which they would have priority rights

Dramatic folding exposes Proterozoic beds on Ellesmere Island. Photo provided by Sproule Associates.

for the award of permits. There were no fees applied to these prior claims. Dominion Explorers and Round Valley Oil sent geological field parties to the islands that summer, and Sproule and others spent that first year conducting photogeological work.

Gordon Jones, who set up the photogeology department at Sproule, was initially working with trimetrogon photos. Much of the work in the field later on was verifying and sampling geological structures interpreted from the photographs. Gordon remarked:

> When flying reconnaissance, one could see abundant outcrops from the aircraft, but when one got on the ground, there could be nothing but piles of frost-heaved rubble, rendering readings of dip and strike useless. One had to take pains to use fine-tuned photogeology to make it corroborate with field observations.

In April of 1960, regulations were developed. Each permit cost $250 plus a deposit of five cents an acre to guarantee work of that same value was carried out on the permit during the first three-year period. Once sufficient credits toward that work were accumulated, the money was refunded.

Drilling expenses were given double the credits. Work commitments increased after the first three years—15 cents per acre for three years, then 20 cents per acre for two years—and at the end of 12 years, permits terminated and leases would have to be obtained before production was allowed.

Another set of regulations existed for leases. They required Canadian content for companies during the development stage: the companies had to be listed on the Canadian stock exchange or have majority Canadian control. "Stipulations in the 1960 regulations militated against the multinational companies in favor of the small independents," said Max Foran in a presentation to the Western Studies Conference in 1983, "thus reversing the earlier trend which had seen the multi-nationals dominate exploration in the Mackenzie Basin."

Considered unsatisfactory by some, the regulations were adjusted the following year, though 50 percent Canadianization continued to be mandatory.

In June 1960, with regulations in place, the "rush" was on. The *Daily Oil Bulletin* (June 24, 1960) reported:

> Reliable sources in Ottawa today informed the Daily Oil Bulletin that up to 10:00 a.m. (Ottawa Time), Friday, Arctic Island filing had reached near the 37,000,000 acre mark.
>
> There is expected to be quite a last-minute rush today as application for priority rights close at 4:00 p.m. EDT, or 1:00 p.m. Calgary time. Application for open permits after today will be processed on a first-come, first-served basis on July 4th, 1960.

Ice covers the frigid waters of Makinson Inlet, Ellesmere Island. Photo provided by Sproule Associates.

Forty-five million acres were leased in the 1960 rush; by November of 1963, that number had grown to 55 million. By 1966, some 63 million acres in the Islands had been leased under Canadian regulations to exploration firms. Most were small, independent Canadian companies and individuals, but there were a few large companies as well, including California Standard, Texaco Exploration, and Union Oil. Shell Oil also controlled a large block, and other relatively large holdings were filed by Pan Arctic Syndicate (the Joseph Hirshhorn interests), Bankeno Mines, Canadian Amco Limited, Dominion Explorers, and Round Valley Oil. According to *The Oil and Gas Journal* (July 25, 1966), the Pan Arctic Syndicate, for whom Sproule was doing work, controlled about 70 percent of it.

According to Stan Kanik, one of the administrators of the regulations, the distribution of oil and gas rights in the Arctic was on a first-come first-served basis. Creation of Crown reserves on the discovery of oil and gas recognized the remoteness of the area and, in the early years, gave the original permittee, now lessee, the first right to acquire the Crown reserve corridor acreage on a gross overriding royalty percent. Each permit covered an area of 50,000 acres, enclosed by 30 minutes of longitude and 10 minutes of latitude. There was no requirement to make a discovery to be able to convert the permit to lease. It could be converted at any time, but the costs were onerous—one dollar per acre. By far, the greatest amount of credit was earned by drilling of wells, though geophysical and geological work also earned points.

Initially, the exploration programs confined themselves almost entirely to the work commitments dictated by the amounts of the deposits required by the Crown to hold the permit acreage in good standing. Some of the permit lands were dropped after the first three years, but most of the prospective lands were held for a second three-year period. The regulations also provided for the auctioning of lands. There was a substantial amount of land that permittees would abandon when they ran out of money. To avoid losing permitted lands, the government allowed the permittee to come back the next morning and re-file on the same lands. Numbers were put in a hat and the permittees hoped their number would come up. The cost was $250 per permit and five cents an acre for 18 months.

A helicopter touches down for a preliminary surface survey inside Barrow Dome, Sabine Peninsula, Melville Island. Photo provided by Sproule Associates.

Selling Arctic Exploration

Cam differed from GSC geologists in his perspective, though he was always interested in the purely scientific side of exploration. Nate Peterson, a Sproule geologist, commended him for being thorough and innovative when it came to the geological work:

> The concept of producing stratigraphic sections complete with cuttings was unique. It meant some serious work in the outcrop. The concept of going in and mapping entire basins, rather than focusing on a specific client's acreage, was a credit to him.

Cam's goal in geological exploration was resource development. In a paper published in *Geology of the Arctic* in 1961, he wrote that technical and scientific information concerning the Arctic

> are of no use to humanity if they do not lead to an economic evaluation of the Arctic as a human habitation and/or as an area from which the human race can derive benefits in the form of the gainful production of natural resources.

Cam was probably the biggest and most vocal advocate of Arctic exploration, quick to point out that operations there are relatively inexpensive. Vast amounts of information were available from previous GSC expeditions and aerial photographs, so the search for prospective oil and gas structures was made easier. The *Daily Oil Bulletin* (May 20, 1960) reported:

> The average preliminary exploratory costs on the mainland have varied from four to five cents per acre, whereas detailed preliminary work is being done on the islands for between one and one-half cents per acre and a maximum of two cents per acre, depending upon the size and accessibility of the project acreage. The related regional structural, stratigraphic, and facies work is being done for an additional one and one-half cents per (permit) acre.

Cam also showed that detailed surface studies could be easily undertaken on the substantially exposed outcrops found along creeks and

"This is the largest untapped potential oil basin in the Western Hemisphere."
Photo provided by the Sproule family.

60

escarpments. The general lack of precipitation meant little transport of surface material, so much of the debris (most of the terrain is covered by rubble of disintegrated bedrock) reflected the underlying formation. Over most of the Western Canadian Sedimentary Basin area, deep drilling operations through substantial overburden were required (often involving large sums of money) to obtain similar stratigraphic information. In an article published in *The Albertan* (September 25, 1961) Cam said, "If the industry were to enter the area on a fair scale, it could find oil at a very low cost compared, for example, with expenditures incurred over most basin areas in Western Canada." This didn't mean that the drilling of exploratory deep wells would not be necessary at all, but that operators could progress far beyond the stage at which these wells were commonly drilled. Because of the close relationship of the Arctic Islands to the Canadian Precambrian Shield and the Western Canadian Sedimentary Basin, previous knowledge, especially of the latter, would be of great value in assessing the oil and gas prospects of the Islands.

A real plus in Arctic Islands exploration in Cam's mind was that much of the terrain was flat and suitable for landing light fixed-wing aircraft. The permafrost receded only a few inches beneath the surface during the summer, and the overlying thin layers of soft, wet alluvium and soil were generally navigable. Cam suggested that when the time came for heavy freight transport, special tracked or large-wheeled vehicles would serve well. More important, the cost of transportation by air was far lower than by sea, the only alternative. The *Daily Oil Bulletin* (May 20, 1960) reported that Sproule's first move into the Arctic, contracted to Territorial Bulk Distributors (who used a stripped DC4) cost under $10,000:

> This freight rate is about half the price charged by competing transporters, who also offer passenger service into the north, and if profitable for the contractor, could be a major boon to exploration companies. This rate is actually cheaper than that paid by the same consulting firm for delivery of supplies into field areas in the lower Mackenzie area on previous survey operations.

At the same time, the limited payloads of the aircraft required that the exploration parties travel light, and costs for supplies, and their transport, were indirectly reduced.

The costs of drilling were estimated to be not much more than in the south, assuming that drilling on the islands could be conducted over a full 12 months a year because of the absence of muskeg or swamps. In the northern parts of Alberta and British Columbia, and in the southern parts of the Northwest Territories, drilling was undertaken on a four- to five-month basis. In the article in *The Albertan* Cam said: "As a result of our improved knowledge of the geology of the Arctic, it is safe to say that the incidence of discovery per well drilled will be high and finding cost of oil on a per-barrel basis is bound to be low."

Overcoming the Downside

Cam, like others, recognized the two biggest hurdles to Arctic Island resource development—transportation and markets—but was not discouraged by them. Though ice limited marine transport to about three months of the year (except for the eastern islands bordering Baffin Bay, where navigation was possible for about eight months of the year), he was confident that needed transportation technology was imminent. "The islands are only inaccessible on a basis of presently inadequate transportation facilities," he said in an article published in *Oilweek* (May 21, 1962):

> If the incentive were present it should not take science long to devise icebreakers that could move more or less at will through the Arctic Islands for at least the greater part of the year. Science has accomplished so much in our generation that the development of such mechanical equipment would be classed only as a minor scientific success. Meanwhile, the idea of effective and economical large-scale submarine freight traffic is so far advanced as to be practically assured within the next five to eight years.

During the 1940s and 1950s, shipping into the Arctic *had* become more practical—several voyages through the Northwest Passage, and under-ice voyages by nuclear submarines, had taken place. He spoke about a new invention in a presentation to the Canadian Institute of Surveying in January 1968:

> The recent development of "Alexbow," an ice-plow that has already been tried during the winter in ice-bound Lake Ontario and which is now employed in further experimental work by the U.S. Coast Guard in the Chicago River, promises ultimately to overcome the problem of moving marine craft through normal Arctic ice conditions, either in winter or summer. When this takes place, it is not difficult to imagine what it will do, not only to the opening of the northern part of this

Cam stands on an ice flow in Resolute Bay, with the ice-breaker C.D. Howe *in the background. Photo provided by Gordon Jones.*

Continent but to Canada's position in the World Transportation picture. To cite only one example, we might point out that the distance from Tokyo to the British Isles area by way of Bering Strait and the Polar Ice Cap is about 7,000 miles whereas the distance between the same two points by way of the Panama Canal is nearly 14,000 miles.

Nuclear submarine "super" tanker designs were touted as possible answers to future mineral transportation, and Cam was an ardent supporter of the concept. "This was at a time when support for such an idea earned at best polite smiles and scepticism," wrote Jim Stott of the *Calgary Herald* (September 29, 1972). Stott was reporting on the results of a study of the feasibility of underwater barges pulled by surface icebreakers, undertaken by Continental Oil Company.

In 1970, the year of Cam Sproule's death, the *S.S. Manhattan* showed that an ice-breaking supertanker could do the job.

Cam believed the logical market for Arctic oil was northern Europe, given the shorter transportation distance from the Islands than from the Middle East, which was currently supplying them. He also suggested that Japan and the Atlantic and Pacific seaboards, in addition to the interior of Canada, would be good future prospects, and he pointed out that the mining of Arctic mineral resources would create an additional market.

There was a natural overlap of areas holding promise for hydrocarbon discovery with areas of metallic mineral prospects, so, predictably, J.C. Sproule and Associates got into mineral and other natural

---

The Alexbow

The Alexbow was an ice plow that broke up ice cover from below, rather than riding down on its surface from above, as other ice-breakers did. The inventor, Scott Alexander, claimed that a ship equipped with his ice plow, capable of travelling 16 knots in open water, could plow through six or more feet of ice at a speed of 10 knots.

The Alexbow was attached to the front end of a ship much like a snow plow on the front of a railway locomotive. It was essentially a flared plow with a splinter blade that produced a splitting action. It protruded under the surface, attacking the ice from its softer underbelly, and used the buoyancy of the ship to break the ice up. One-twelfth as much energy was required to break up the ice cover by this upward thrust as compared to a downward thrust, according to Alexander. The largest ice-breaking ships in use at the time could plow through no more than three feet of ice at a speed of about one knot, by attempting to ram the ice down into the water. The mean average thickness of the polar ice was only five feet, apparently well within the capability of a ship equipped with the Alexbow. The upward thrust of the Alexbow broke the ice into smaller pieces and "mush," which was deposited on top of the ice pack on either side of the path, leaving a clear channel behind. Conventional ice-breaking ships left large chunks of ice in their wake, which were a menace to any following ships.

In a Calgary meeting of oil men involved in Panarctic Oils' exploration program, Alexander said a 50,000-ton tanker, designed to operate year-round through polar ice, could be built in two years, at a cost of $18 million. An agreement between Panarctic and Alexbow Ltd. was referred to in the Daily Oil Bulletin *(July 18, 1968)* whereby Alexbow Canada Limited was formed; it was owned 51 percent by Panarctic and 49 percent by Alexbow Ltd.

A letter from Alexbow Ltd. to Panarctic Oils' shareholders (including the estate of Cam Sproule), dated October 9, 1973, reported that a full-scale Alexbow was built in 1970 and tested in thin freshwater ice. The test was disappointing, because the channel behind the vehicle wasn't clear of ice. Structural changes (addition of wings to the plow) were proposed. Further, model tests in test-tank ice suggested the Alexbow took more horsepower for a given amount of ice than the conventional ice-breaker. Nevertheless, the advantages—namely, a clear channel behind—were believed to outweigh this.

More research was believed required, but Panarctic Oils was apparently not willing to invest more. Alexbow Ltd. was experiencing financial difficulties and was requesting $1 per share from shareholders to cover its current costs.

According to Grey Alexander of Panarctic Oils (former director of Alexbow), the plow was never produced, or used, commercially.

S.S. Manhattan

In August 1969, Humble Oil & Refining Company, the U.S. operating arm of Standard Oil of New Jersey, sent the S.S. Manhattan, *a 1,004-foot, 155,000-ton supertanker reinforced for ice-breaking, on an 8,000-mile journey from New York to Prudhoe Bay, Alaska and back. They wanted to see not only if it could be done, but if shipping by tanker made more economic sense for moving Alaska's north shore oil to the United States east coast via the Northwest Passage than building a 3,500-mile pipeline across North America. The* S.S. Manhattan *"adventure," as it was called by Earle Gray in* Oilweek *(October 16, 1995), culminated a 500-year quest for a commercial shipping route across "the top of the world."*

The ship was accompanied by Canadian Coast Guard ice-breaker John A. MacDonald *and United States ice-breaker* Northwind. *The operation proved feasible, although pack-ice brought the ship to a standstill several times, forcing it to reroute. Nevertheless, the cost savings were less than expected, and arguments in favour of the pipeline were made, including less risk of serious pollution by large accidental oil spills. In addition, the pipeline could provide market access for oil reserves found inland throughout northern Canada.*

The ice-breaking supertanker idea was not a bust, for it also provided a passage for oil shipments out of the eastern sector of Canada's Arctic Islands, with their even larger potential reserves of crude oil. Shipping oil out of Canada's eastern Arctic avoided 1,500 miles of ice-clogged water, reducing the exposure to ice to between 100 and 500 miles. The economics of ice-breaking across these lesser distances was much more attractive. All that was needed was a prolific discovery or two in Canada's eastern Arctic.

resource exploration and development in the Arctic Islands. Cam spoke to the Association of Professional Engineers of Alberta and the Engineering Institute of Canada in 1967, citing a considerable variety of minerals found in sedimentary, igneous, and metamorphic rock in Western Canada and, by implication, in the Arctic Islands. While carrying out surveys on Little Cornwallis Island during the 1960 field season, Sproule geologist Lionel Singleton discovered a lead-zinc deposit on oil and gas exploratory permits of Bankeno Mines. The find turned out to be a deposit of exceptional size and grade, and is part of what is now known as the Cornwallis Lead-Zinc District. Drilling in 1971 revealed the large extent of the deposit. Another spectacular mineral showing was found on nearby Truro Island, and both deposits were developed by Cominco. Pre-production ore reserves were estimated to be about 23 million tons of 4.3 percent lead and 14.1 percent zinc. As Cam said in *Oilweek* (December 18, 1967):

> There are few other large areas on earth where such a happy geographic relationship exists between metallic mineral resources and readily available and relatively inexpensive sources of hydrocarbon energy with which to develop the reserves.

In his position as president of the Canadian Institute of Mining and Metallurgy (CIM), Cam promoted cooperation between the oil and gas industry and metallic minerals industry (as well as research and government) and the advantages to be gained from that cooperation. Not only would mutual transportation facilities and services cut costs for both, but establishing metallic industries would create markets for the oil and gas industry, helping to finance the latter's exploration work. In addition, both industries would benefit from the presence of cheap sources of fuel. He encouraged cooperation, in an article published in *Oilweek* (January 16, 1960):

> Those concerned with development of both metallic and non-metallic mineral resources would do well to get together in their planning to lighten the burden for both groups. Authorities agree that the area is rich in natural resources and that it is merely a question of time and technical know-how. Why wait 50 years if we can do it in 25 years? Why wait 25 years if we can do it in 10 years?

Cam was often frustrated by the pace at which development occurred in the Arctic, and he held strong views about foreign investment, as indicated in an article published in *Oilweek* (October 15, 1962):

> It is unfortunate that principal interest in the Arctic is confined to independents who have the strength, but may not have the faith to proceed on a reasonable scale. And a lot of these independents are Canadian companies, and it's notorious that Canadians don't spend Canadian money in Canada.

> It might be as well for some of our politicos to remember this when they talk of stemming the tide of foreign investment in Canada—Canadian money probably won't be forthcoming to fill the gap.

> Canadians are very timid about investing in Canada. If the Arctic Islands are to be developed it will probably be done by United States' or other foreign money.

In fact, Petropar Canada Ltd., a company essentially controlled by the French government, came to be the largest single permit holder in the

Mineralization provides a show of colour at the lead-zinc discovery site on Little Cornwallis Island, 1960. Photo provided by Sproule Associates.

Ice meets rock on Ellesmere Island. Photo provided by Sproule Associates.

Arctic Islands. Said Cam Sproule in a paper published by the International Oil Scouts Association and cited in the *Calgary Herald* (June 26, 1965):

> The natural conclusion we would come to is that Petropar may not be seriously worried either about markets or transportation. When they do find it and produce it and find a market for it, let us not hear any complaints from Canadian politicos or others about foreign control. If it were not for this and other so-called foreign control of operations in Canada in the past, principally by the United States, the Western Canadian oil business would be, at this time, practically non-existent.

In an article in *The Albertan* (September 21, 1961) he said:

> If industry were to get behind the development of the Arctic Islands on a reasonable scale, we believe it would be capable of producing oil commercially within about five years. But, if for some reason or other, a sufficient portion of industry did not enter the area, economic developments could be delayed for a number of years.

In a paper published in *Canadian Oil and Gas Industries* in 1961, Cam wrote about the importance of major oil companies getting on board because they were best equipped to develop the oil resources of the Arctic Islands. He recognized that it was in their best interests to spend their money on known reserves in other parts of the world, where it was relatively inexpensive to produce, but he cautioned that assuming Arctic oil would still be there to exploit 25 years later was dangerous:

> The land area of Canada is greater than that of the United States, whereas our population is less than one-tenth that of the United States. Canada is rich in natural resources and we might be expected to be satisfied to develop slowly and methodically, limited in the magnitude of our effort only by our own resources. If that policy is followed, however, in our opinion it could be fifty to one hundred years before the Arctic is opened up on a reasonable scale. The only alternative to that procedure appears to be to invite foreign money to assist in the development of Canada, including the Arctic Islands, under conditions that encourage expenditure of such funds, without placing our

resources entirely under the control of foreign powers. This could mean revisions of present tax laws to encourage foreign companies to incorporate in Canada and help develop the country as "New Canadians."

Gaining a Foothold

Cam viewed the Arctic Islands as another Middle East in terms of its oil and gas potential. In a presentation to the CIM (cited in *Oilweek*, May 21, 1962), Sproule said: "The Arctic Islands is the only place in Canada and probably the only place on earth where an independent oil company has a chance to become a major oil company." He pursued his clients and sold the idea to them, pointing out two further significant advantages to moving into the Arctic Islands: Crown ownership of land (as opposed to privately held mineral titles) simplified large-scale exploration for mineral resources, and there was a strong desire of the federal government to develop northern Canada. The International Symposium on Arctic Geology, held in Calgary in January 1960, stimulated further professional interest. As Bob Armstrong, a Cominco employee at the time, remarked: "One couldn't talk to Sproule and fly over the Arctic and not see huge oil deposits. He was a great salesman who really believed in his product—it was the 'sincere' part that sold people."

Cam provided detailed recommendations for permit filing to clients, such as Pan Arctic Syndicate, and when the exploration permit "dust" had settled, Sproule was taking care of a substantial proportion of the acreage involved, for clients of various sizes. In the first five years, very few put their own field parties in the Arctic Islands; almost all chose to use consultants, and Sproule had 80 to 90 percent of the work.

Doc Sproule finally gives in. Photo provided by Bert Ellison.

Rein de Wit remarked: "Cam seemed to have a nose for sniffing out the best areas." He had no more information than was available to anyone, but had a "by guess or by gosh" approach. Fred Roots, formerly with the GSC, said Cam was happiest talking about what was happening to the big sedimentary basins and movement of the continents, and he had a feel for which were the important parts of the country to look at and which weren't.

Working in the Arctic Islands

Sproule field parties first set foot in the Arctic in the spring of 1960, after a year of studying and mapping the Islands' geology using the photos taken by the military. The geologists also reviewed in detail the reports written by the GSC (and carried many of them with them into the Arctic). They worked for many clients over most of the central Queen Elizabeth Islands. Round Valley Oil, Dominion Explorers, and Imperial Oil were the only others doing geological exploratory work on the Islands that season. The GSC was also there, as was a large Polar Continental Shelf research group.

Operations in the Arctic were less affected by weather than one would think, but it was definitely a factor. Temperatures there were cool for the three-month summer and cold for the nine-month winter. The mean annual temperature on the Islands was about -6°F, with a winter low of -60°F and a summer high of about +58°F. The large volume of water, even though it was frozen during most of the year, moderated the climate so that extreme low temperatures were not as severe as expected at that latitude.

There was complete darkness for three months and complete daylight for three months. But precipitation was low in the winter and summer—the average annual in some areas, exclusive of the mountains, being 2.5 inches. Glaciers covered about eight percent of the land area of the Islands, but during the summer, with low precipitation and 24 hours of sunlight, most Island areas were clear of snow.

Strong winds and fog were prevalent in the summer, and proved the greatest hindrance to aircraft—they apparently weren't that pleasant for the field crews either. Gordon Jones, Sproule's chief photogeologist in the first several Arctic field seasons, recalls: "Rime (heavy frost) in thicknesses as great as six inches formed on the ropes during 60-knot winds on Vanier Island, northwest of Bathurst Island. These winds were so violent that they would blow the tents away." Bryce Cameron wrote in 1983 that the men always had their sleeping bags and parkas with them, whether they were just taking a short flight or walking from camp, because they could easily get trapped by fog.

> Other pieces of equipment that you should have are sunglasses, toques or balaclavas, scarves, two pairs of gloves, shirts, pullovers, thick trousers, several pairs of socks or stockings, ordinary shoes and overboots. Also, and I nearly forgot, long johns or pants woollen long, as they were called in my British Army days.

Cam called the Arctic Islands "cold deserts surrounded by ice-bound seas," although stunted vegetation was widespread for certain parts of the year, supporting herds of muskox and caribou, lemmings and rabbits, and consequently, weasels, wolverines, and other predators. A sparse but widely distributed bird population was also supported, and the geological parties saw plenty of fox and wolf, and of course, polar bear.

In the 1962 field season on King Christian Island, helicopter pilot Bob O'Conner and helicopter engineer Howie Carmichael had a close encounter with a polar bear while camped with a geologist and his assistant at a "fly camp." Usually, each camp was provided a rifle, according to Stan Harding, but they were without one. At 4:30 A.M. (24-hour daylight at this time), Bob and Howie sensed something tripping on their tent strings. Stan tells the story:

> Bob is looking for a flare while Howie, who always slept in his birthday suit, is out of his sleeping bag and on his knees. He sees the polar bear's nose through the sailcloth, against the front of the tent, and its big paw up, ready to rip the tent apart. Instinctively, Howie punches the polar bear in the nose as hard as he can, and tells him where to go! And he went. Meanwhile, Bob has a flare ready and sticks it out the front of the tent and pokes his head out and sees two bears! There is blood all over the front of the tent, but the bear has backed off. When Howie realized what he had done, he was shaking so hard he couldn't get his clothes on, and swore he was through with the Arctic for good! But the next year he was back.

A five-inch plate of ice forms on half-inch tie-down rope after eight days of blowing freezing fog. Vanier Island. Photo provided by Sproule Associates.

Sproule exploration and mapping parties to the Arctic Islands varied in number and size. The *Daily Oil Bulletin* heralded Sproule's first field season in 1960, reporting that the initial party comprised four geologists, a geological assistant, a cook, and two pilots, but that Sproule was prepared to put 12 to 14 "geological units" into the field. In the 1961 field season, four parties were sent on behalf of numerous clients, led by Rein de Wit, Don Campbell, Stan Harding, and Jack Usher and consisting of eight, twelve, nine, and fourteen persons, respectively.

Photogeology

In the initial air surveys of the Arctic by the Canadian government shortly after the war, a technique known as trimetrogon air photography was used. Three cameras were installed in the floor of an airplane: one was adjusted to take vertical photos while the other two, on either side, took oblique photos, to the left and right of the flight line. The obliques overlapped the vertical photos, all three being taken continuously to provide a complete view of the ground from one horizon to the other. Each oblique photo overlapped the vertical one, but according to Bryce Cameron, only the portion representing about 18 miles on either side of the vertical was of use. About 36 miles was covered on a given flight line, so coverage of an area was cheaper and quicker than using purely vertical shots, which were done after 1958.

A vertical photographic survey involved only one camera in the floor of the plane, each photo covering about 70 square miles, so a plane was flown at a constant height along parallel courses to provide overlap of the courses of about 30 percent. The flight lines could be 5½ miles apart. Given the nature of flying, only very skilled and experienced pilots could produce a good set of photos.

Simply put, the vertical photos were then used to form a mosaic by gluing them to firm paper, with all overlapping areas cut off. (The edges of the photos have the greatest distortion.) The end result is a photo map of an area.

The overlaps between the photos allowed stereoscopic studies to be made of the terrain. A three-dimensional effect is created when two photos taken of the same object from different positions are held in front of the eyes, such that one appears superimposed on the other. Features displaying height and breadth stand out in relief. A pair of overlapping photos is a stereopair and the instrument used for examining them, a stereoscope. Cameron wrote in 1983:

> When one views a pair of photographs by using such an instrument the resulting impression can be quite uncanny. One imagines one can actually touch that snow covered peak displayed before you or swim down that gently flowing river. All objects stand out and appear alive.

At J.C. Sproule and Associates, photomosaics occupied everyone's time at one point or another. According to Zoltan Zalan, who was in charge of the process, photos were grouped so that areas would fit on a maximum 4x8-foot board. The original flight line was built by stapling photos together that shared one identical point and points at the edges lined up to form a straight line. These were stapled to the board.

For photos that were 6x6 inches, and assuming a 30 percent overlap, 18 to 24 photos could fit on the board in one direction (say, east to west); from north to south, approximately 8 to 12 flight lines fit on the board. Using existing government topographic maps of the area, a mean land elevation was determined (the photomap was scaled). Accuracy was extremely important, because the government maps were then sent out and copied at the new scale. They would become the base maps upon which the final product was laid.

The base maps were spliced together and stapled on a softer temporary board. The original reconstructed flight lines were taken apart and stapled temporarily onto the base maps, each illustrating major features in their proper place.

The photos were marked for trimming, with adjustments made where necessary to accommodate each flight line, then numbered and cross-referenced on the maps, and removed from the board. The photos were then feathered, that is, scored just the right amount, and the edges removed. This took great skill, because too much cutting could lead to curled edges, and too little to thick edges, which would show up as black lines on the final product.

The base maps were transferred and stapled to a harder board, and the photos were re-laid and stapled as indicated by the cross-references. Final adjustments were made, and the board, with information regarding units into which the board had been divided, was provided to film lab technicians.

Different mosaics could be joined up using a process that was equally meticulous. The final product was coloured at the Sproule offices by Sproule staff, each colour representing the outcrop of a different formation. An overlay would be used to cover the new photomosaic and the outline of a particular formation carefully cut out of it. Then the formation was painted. This process was repeated for each formation to be coloured. In some cases, if the complete map could be interpreted, the entire photomosaic was coloured.

Field, permit, and regional geological mapping was carried out for clients such as TriCeeTee, Canadian Amco, and the Pan Arctic Syndicate on Banks, Victoria, Melville, Prince Patrick, and Bathurst Islands, as well as others. Weather conditions were exceptionally bad that summer. Party No. 3 reported:

> During the first half of July, eleven out of fifteen days may be classified as bad to very bad (snow blizzard, freezing fog, dense fog—sometimes accompanied by winds) and only four can be classified as fair (light fog, brief snow squalls, light winds, dull overcast and occasional sunny intervals).

Despite conditions, the 1961 Sproule exploration of the Arctic Islands was the largest in scope and area ever covered in the Arctic by one single company. *The Albertan* (September 25, 1961) wrote:

> This latest expedition filled important gaps in the knowledge about the area, confirmed, broadened and deepened experiences gained in earlier explorations and laid the groundwork for further trips into the Arctic.
>
> Beginning in June this year, the company conducted detailed field exploration of permit areas for 16 clients covering almost the entire Arctic Islands basin, continued last year's exploratory work, conducted local detailed work and started reconnaissance in new areas.
>
> The team of experts was divided into four groups comprising 16 mapping units, each covering a large area. The work was supported by a total of 16 aircraft on a full or part-time basis.

Sproule field parties consisted of geologists and university staff familiar with the geology of the Western Canadian Sedimentary Basin, students, cooks, pilots, and aircraft engineers. The "employee" numbers at Sproule tended to "explode" in the summer. All parties were supported by fixed-wing aircraft (such as the Piper Cub, Beaver, Helio Courier,

A Sproule camp is set up on Melville Island. Photo provided by Sproule Associates.

and others) and Bell helicopters. Fixed-wing aircraft had oversized wheels, which allowed them to land on soft ground.

The most economic exploration unit was governed by the "double plane" party. The two planes were provided as a safety measure, and the size of the unit was governed by the most efficient use of the aircraft and the camp facilities. In a 1960 letter to William Newman, of J.H. Hirshhorn Enterprises, Cam wrote:

> The nature of the operation is such that a great deal of stratigraphic study work, involving voluminous notes and a fair amount of current mapping is advisable. It will, therefore, be necessary for the Party Chiefs to spend a part of their time in the field office. If there were only two Seniors on a party the aircraft would be idle a fair percentage of the time.

And he insisted that each party be provided a cook:

> With reference to the matter of a cook, we realize that many field parties in the Precambrian and in the far North reduce the size of their party operations by doing without a cook, in the interests of economy. We believe, on the other hand, that cooks added to these parties will greatly add to their economy and efficiency, inasmuch as time is not wasted by field geologists in attending to unnecessary camp duties, when the party includes a full-time cook. The limited summer work period that is involved means that every geologist should work at top speed in order to produce at maximum efficiency. He cannot do this if he is cooking two or three meals a day and attending to other camp duties.
>
> It has been our experience after many years of geological exploration work that a cook on a party of more than about three adds greatly to the efficiency of the party.

The parties set up numerous camps over the course of the field season, both base camps and "fly camps." In the latter case, small teams, usually two-man, camped "on the rocks" in areas remote from base camps, and they would work for a week to 10 days. They were provided emergency supplies in case the weather deteriorated or an airplane breakdown prevented pick-up at the previously agreed time.

Stan Harding takes a well-earned rest. Photo provided by Sproule Associates.

Wally Drew described the Sproule camps as "Spartan" compared to the oil company camps: "One time we were doing a traverse, ending at Mobil's camp. They had a real luxury there—a toilet—with a real toilet seat on top and a shelter around it!" The first field season, in 1960, saw a great deal of dehydrated food. "The ground beef was one of our staples," said Gordon Jones, "and it sort of tasted something like sawdust. It really was very hard to make it palatable." Cam's daughter Judy recalled her father "in orbit" when Gordon McCracken, as expediter, ordered sirloin steaks: the cost of shipping food north was "astronomical."

The parties were usually divided into four or five units, often camping and working apart from each other, ensuring that some work might be done by some units even if others were hampered by weather. Even under poor conditions, some kinds of work, such as measuring and sampling, could be done. Lost working hours due to weather conditions were offset by working long hours during good weather, and even working all night when warranted. Cam hated to see the crews idle. Gordon Jones remarked: "There were long periods of enforced grounding due to bad weather. Sproule endured these periods, but he just couldn't stand to see anybody sitting around. This included the cook, who he got to dig trenches for drainage—a totally useless effort." Sproule geologist Bob Workum said Cam arranged for four months' work in the 1960 field season: "But there were really only six or seven good weeks in the field, because of snow cover and weather conditions. As far as Sproule was concerned, if he could get a geologist on the ground, there was work that could be done!" Gordon said that three months in the Arctic was the norm, at least in theory, though they were usually slogging around in snow the first two or three weeks and the last two or

A Sproule fly camp is home for geologists working on Svendsen Peninsula, Ellesmere Island. Photo provided by Sproule Associates.

three. According to geologist Hank Roessingh, crews were out by the first week of September, before the weather changed. "It was known that it wasn't safe to stay out there beyond a certain time, because of the white-outs." White-outs were particularly dangerous for flying.

Working with aircraft in the North was not without difficulties. The biggest hurdle was always weather. "Fog or wind could hamper, or make impossible, planned flights," said Gordon:

If you just happen to hit the slightest change in temperature, it makes it almost impossible to know if you are flying up-side-down or right-side-up—it's just a very dangerous condition. One could say that most of the pilots flew beyond their skills. They were daredevils, but they also used wisdom and judgement.

On the whole, we got on without too many bad accidents. We damaged a lot of aircraft and not too many people. We had a lot of scares, and I guess my nerves for flying have not been too good after so many episodes. There were many times when you got above the clouds, and we were flying aircraft with visual flight rules, which means in theory we should never be above the clouds. But sometimes the clouds would form below you while you were up in the air; then you would have to find a way down and hope there was a gap in the clouds somewhere. Sometimes we would fly over a camp that we knew to be there, and people would talk us down by radio. At least they could tell us if there was a space under the clouds and they weren't sitting right on top of the hills.

Hank Roessingh remembers flipping a Beaver on take-off at the end of the summer of 1963. The plane was badly damaged and he worked with the mechanic to dismantle it so that it could be removed in pieces. "You couldn't leave the pieces of a broken Beaver in the field."

In the summer, flights were over open water that usually had ice floating in it. Gordon said that the pilots couldn't fly

A blizzard grounds the aircraft on Isachsen Peninsula, Ellef Ringnes Island. Photo provided by Gordon Jones.

too low. "You had absolutely no earthly hope of surviving if the engine started coughing, so it was best to stay at maximum height and within gliding distance of an island." Remarked Stan Harding, "We didn't bother wearing life jackets, because we figured if we were ever down in the water, we wouldn't last long anyway."

Tragedy did strike Sproule in the Arctic: geologist Allan Reece and pilot Harcourt Papst were killed in a crash in 1960 while doing preliminary surveying. "Rather a bleak start for our Arctic Islands fieldwork," said Stan.

Photos provided by Sproule Associates.

Arctic Tragedy

Our aircraft had arrived only a couple of days before; Harcourt Papst and Bill Robertson had brought the two Piper Super Cubs up. Russ Bradley, of Bradley Air Services, was also in camp with a third Piper. They had to service the aircraft after the trip up, and then we thought we had some good enough weather to fly. Reece and Papst were going to fly up the east side of Cornwallis Island and look for a place to camp on the north end of the Island. They were going to do a general reconnaissance, and the other aircraft was made available to Bill Robertson and either Bob Workum or me. We flipped a coin, and Bob won the toss and he went out in the second aircraft, checking out the geology on the east coast of Cornwallis Island, which was still 98 percent snow-covered. Neither one of the planes came back that night.

Early the following morning, I went to Bradley and I said, "Those guys aren't back yet. They were intending to be back last night. I think we'd better go and take a look for them. I think it's time to start a search now." Bradley agreed, so he and I went out and flew most of the day. We flew up the east side of the Island. Near Read Bay we saw one aircraft on the ice, and it obviously had damaged its undercar-

riage. So we landed near it, and I half-jokingly said to Bob Workum, "You're out without permission and no late pass." He said, "What do you mean?" and I said, "Well, we're a little concerned; we didn't know where you were." And he said, "Didn't Reece and Papst tell you?" I knew then there was a problem. I said, "No, were they here?" Robertson and Workum's plane had had a bad landing. They broke the landing gear and the wings and the radio. There was ice up through the floor. Reece and Papst had showed up a couple of hours later, had landed and had headed off across the Island to get help—as near as we can tell, straight back for Resolute Bay. But they never got there.

Bradley and I started a search, but we couldn't search the interior of the Island—there were snow storms and white-outs, and at that stage we had only one aircraft. We couldn't let it get bogged down in case it was needed to help others who were in trouble. We searched any place where the weather was reasonably good, and finally Bradley was starting to get a little tired at being at the controls, so he and I got out of the Piper, and a chap named Dick Debliquy took off with another fellow and found some clearer weather, and the aircraft. I think he landed near it, then came back and said both guys

had been killed. By that time, we had a Beaver to use, and I went out with two policemen and Dick Debliquy to retrieve the bodies.

It wasn't a pleasant affair. It's funny, when I was flying in the air force I saw lots of people getting killed, and I saw lots of people disappearing. I thought I'd built up a shell of indifference, but I discovered that day that my shell of indifference was very thin. It's a risky game, and your own life gets quite precious.

I don't know whether it was a white-out or iced-up instruments that didn't allow them to judge their altitude, but I think the plane crashed under power. There were two right-angle bends in the fuselage. It was squeezed up and Reece wasn't thrown out of the top, although much of his body went out through the top—his feet were trapped in the wreckage so he stayed in the aircraft—and the plane bounced and then rolled and he hit the ground pretty hard. He wouldn't have known what happened to him. It looked to me as though the pilot had lived for a little while, because there was a patch of frozen blood and snow underneath one of his knees; so his heart continued to pump, but I don't know for how long.

George Wilson
Sproule geologist with the 1960 field party

75

The worst air disaster in the Canadian Arctic Islands befell Panarctic Oils in 1973 when pilot error and bad weather resulted in a night crash, just a mile short of Melville Island, approaching Rae Point. Thirty-two people were killed. Only the two pilots survived because the nose cone came off in the crash, and they were able to get out and onto the ice. A cenotaph was erected in memory of those lost.

Because operations of this nature were in their infancy in the Arctic Islands, Cam took a holistic approach to them, organizing and implementing every aspect of it, and making himself personally responsible for it all. As Max Ward, a former Arctic pilot and founder of Wardair, remarked, "He was a no-nonsense pioneer in high Arctic operations when there were few such persons around." Cam, or most often Stan Harding, coordinated field parties with the aid of a radio, from the "Sproule Hut" in Resolute, a permanent steel insulated building built in 1961, at the time a testament to Cam's confidence in the potential of Arctic Islands development. (Cam fell from the roof while installing it, permanently injuring his back, which had already been injured early in his field days.) He did fieldwork occasionally, always as one of the gang. Wally said: "When he came up he would grab a heavy load of rocks and carry them back to camp just like anybody else—he wasn't one to avoid getting his hands dirty."

Though radio reception wasn't always ideal, radios were a life-line for the geological parties camped across the Islands. Hank remembers taking ill once, but a pick-up was delayed because of fog. "There's one thing in the Arctic: everyone listens to the radio all the time, so you know where everybody is and what they're doing. When I finally made it back to Resolute, everybody wanted to know how I was."

A substantial part of the geologists' work was to gather rock samples from the outcrops, every 10 feet according to Hank, to verify what had been interpreted from the aerial photographs:

> We would bag each sample and mark it with a number, then make a pin hole on the photo where the sample had been collected and mark the photo with the number. Samples were ground up in Calgary,

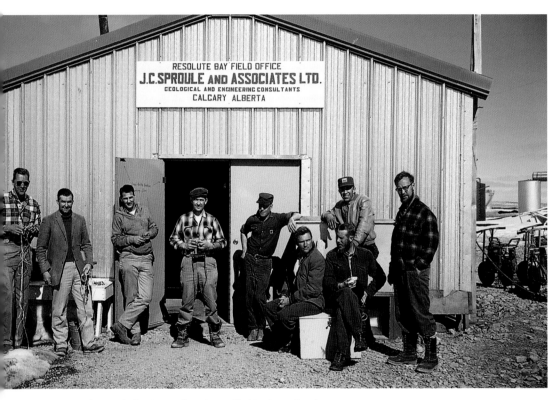

The Sproule "hut" at Resolute, Cornwallis Island provides a base for Arctic operations. Photo provided by Sproule Associates.

in Sproule's ceramics studio, and provided to clients along with their report. They were also sold to others, along with maps and photos, if the samples were relevant to their permit areas.

One interesting problem that arose in the Arctic Islands was that the North Magnetic Pole and magnetic storms rendered the magnetic compass almost useless, and reduced the value of the magnetometer as a geophysical instrument. (The north magnetic pole and true north diverge significantly at that latitude.) It also made flying in the Islands a "little tricky," because compasses in the planes were rendered virtually useless. Gordon Jones pointed this out to Cam, who decided to conduct an experiment one afternoon when they were fogged in at Resolute. "He showed me that his compass always pointed north, and was therefore quite reliable. I assured him it wasn't so—it was pointing north because it was parallel with the plumbing in the building!"

Northward Aviation

The range and efficiency of field studies in the Arctic Islands were greatly expanded by the use of aircraft. Yves Fortier, of the GSC, had chosen the Sikorsky 55 for Operation Franklin in 1955, luring hesitant operators by carefully studying the capabilities of the aircraft as to load and range, and drawing up a circuit map that showed secondary bases to be used away from the main base at Resolute on Cornwallis Island. About halfway between the bases were caches of fuel—shipped by sea in the previous summer, and then distributed the following spring, along with other supplies, by a ski-equipped DC3. Fortier said Okanagan Helicopters of Vancouver, which provided the service, was a major asset in the

Sample bags pile up at Cutthrough Creek Camp, Bathurst Island. Photo provided by Gordon Jones.

success of the operation. They not only dropped geological teams at planned localities, but made untold numbers of unscheduled landings and detours to look more closely at certain geological features viewed from the air. The Survey had found that short take-off and landing aircraft made it possible to carry out survey work at three times the former speed, without increasing costs.

Cam Sproule had also been using aircraft in the mainland of the Northwest Territories. He pointed out that helicopters were useful in moving small field parties from place to place and were well adapted for landing on rough terrain. The rapidly changing Arctic weather conditions, with frequent fog and high winds, had little effect on them, and they were considered a safe means of transportation. Single-engine, fixed-wing aircraft with low-pressure, oversized (DC3) tires were well suited for reconnaissance surveys, and larger models were successfully used for camp moves or for the caching of fuel and other supplies. Hank Roessingh described the process:

> I'd point out a spot on an aerial photograph where I wanted to go. The pilot would fly over it, then around and around, and do a bump landing—touching down and taking off again—until he was satisfied that there weren't too many rocks and it was solid enough so he wouldn't bog down. He would drop us off and go back to the main camp. We'd stay maybe a week before moving on.

It was thus no surprise that Sproule used a lot of aircraft in the Arctic Islands, and that their demand for charter aircraft exceeded the supply, especially on short notice. For Cam Sproule, the solution was simple: buy his own. By 1965, Sproule owned six aircraft, some new from the factory and some used. Some years the company had as many as 17 operating in the Islands. However, the problem with owning them was that the geologists only needed them for three months of the year, during the Arctic field season.

In 1966, Jim Lougheed (uncle of soon-to-be Premier of Alberta, Peter Lougheed) approached Cam and "Doc" Seaman with the possibility that Pacific Western Airlines (PWA) would divest itself of its bush aircraft operations in Northern Alberta and the Northwest Territories. Northward Aviation was incorporated to effect the purchase of some dozen or more aircraft from PWA, including Beavers, Otters, and Cessna 180s and 185s, together with charter bases at Hay Bay, Fort Smith, Yellowknife, Norman Wells, Cambridge Bay, and Inuvik. Sproule Projects Ltd. (Cam's personal holding company) and Seaman's Bow Valley Industries each took about a 30 percent interest in Northward. PWA retained 10 percent, and other financial participants shared the remaining 30 percent. Although Jim Lougheed did not participate in ownership, Northward, by way of consolation, did purchase Lougheed's fleet of two obsolete Norseman aircraft and a WWII-vintage Canso amphibian. These aircraft, together with Sproule's, formed Northward's initial fleet.

The original intention was to achieve year-round use of the aircraft, rather than the three-month field-party use. They offered charters to various companies for the nine months of the year they were not in the field. Sproule's brochure read:

A field-party member prepares for a midnight Beaver flight from Cameron Island fly camp. Photo provided by Bert Ellison.

In Touch with the Past

Gordon Jones stands over the Belcher Expedition's cairn dating to 1852. Photo provided by Sproule Associates.

You would often come across remnants of cairns left by the early explorers. On one particular occasion, we were out working on Devon Island at a place called Cape Majendie. We came across a cairn; it was visible from a long ways away—it was on a real prominent high, near the shore. In that cairn there were messages, in metal canisters, left by Belcher's men looking for Sir John Franklin. These messages were left there in 1852, and they said that they had left supplies down on the beach. There were two canisters, but one had rusted through and there was just pulp in it. The other was perfectly dry, and the message described the stuff left down at the beach. We copied out that message in longhand, put it in another container and put it back in the cairn. We sent the original to the Archives in Ottawa. The following year, Mobil was up there and they also came across this cairn. They took out that message we had left, followed the directions in the message and found cans of beef, canned potatoes, rum, pipes, tobacco...the cans were still in good shape after all those years.

Lionel Singleton

The consultancy controls the full-time use of an Air Division: two engineers, four pilots, two de Havilland Beavers, a Stinson equipped (wheels, floats or skis), two helicopters, a Bell 47G-1 and Bell 47G-3 (both skis and floats). This capability places us in the unique position of being able to take on contract field work anywhere, on short notice.

Said Earl Miller, former treasurer for Sproule:

The hope was that major projects in the northern part of Canada, such as pipelines to bring gas down the Mackenzie River and gas from up in the Arctic Islands, would render Northward a necessity and a financial success. There *were* a number of major projects, but they were never developed, so the future of Northward was certainly not realized by major projects.

For a time, Northward Aviation enjoyed modest success. Its licensing strategically covered the western Territories and Yukon, and so long as oil, gas, and mineral activity held forth the promise of a strong economic base for northern Canada, Northward's future seemed assured. Its modern fleet of turbine-powered Twin Otters, including new Series 300 models CF-JCS and CF-JCH (named after Cam and his wife, Harriet Maude Sproule), was among the largest and best maintained in the Territories.

Unfortunately, Northward was under-capitalized, activity in the far North was negligible during the six winter months, and the new company's "hodgepodge," mainly obsolete fleet did not lend itself to customer requirements nor efficient maintenance back-up. "At the time Sproule died," said Earl, "we were reaching the final stages of the grand field geological–exploration–type parties and evolving into different types of exploration activity, particularly seismic programs and initial exploratory drilling. The demand for field surface parties had started to diminish."

By the end of 1968, Northward's liabilities exceeded its assets, and the company was faced with closure. In characteristic fashion, Cam said, "I don't want my name associated with creditors getting two bits on the dollar," and assigned Tony Edgington and Earl to restructure the ailing Northward. Funding was obtained from the Sproule company; suppliers' accounts were arranged so that all suppliers received full payment within six months; obsolete aircraft were sold; and losing aspects or areas of the operation were shut down. In addition, certain shareholders were bought out, including Bow Valley Industries. Thus, Sproule Projects became the majority shareholder, but at the price of making the consulting firm a guarantor and financier of Northward.

Earl became Northward Aviation's president and ran the company out of Edmonton. Tony acted as executive vice-president, and Noel Cleland served as corporate secretary. The airline flew scheduled flights out of Yellowknife, Whitehorse, and the north country.

The Berger Commission's ten-year moratorium removed any possibility of pipelines to southern Canada, and gradually activity in the Mackenzie valley and delta diminished. Panarctic Oils replaced virtually all other companies in the Arctic Islands and introduced its own aviation division. Thus, Northward was reduced to serving the small Indian and Eskimo communities from PWA's hubs at Inuvik, Yellowknife, Norman Wells, and Cambridge Bay. Although the aggregate mileage of its scheduled routes was the equivalent of New York to Los Angeles, the average population of the communities served was less than 500; most survived on government support. Northward struggled on in this fashion until March 1980, when it was finally forced to shut down. Those Sproule principals still on Northward's board paid off over $100,000 each in bank guarantees.

Icebergs dwarf the field camp in the Van Hauen Pass section of Ellesmere Island. Photo provided by Sproule Associates.

81

When Cam Sproule died in May 1970, the surviving shareholders purchased control of Northward from Sproule Projects. The principal purpose of this transaction was to have the authority and ability to disengage the consulting firm from its involvement in the commercial aviation business, and remove the direct and contingent liabilities from the Sproule Associates balance sheet. Some of the senior associates assumed some obligations personally; certain of the aircraft were sold and leased back directly by Northward, thus removing Sproule from any ongoing liability.

The Outcome: Arctic Oil and Gas

In the summer of 1962, oil-saturated sandstone was discovered in the Marie Bay area of the northwestern part of Melville Island during a normal reconnaissance by a J.C. Sproule and Associates mapping party doing regular gravity readings. "You would never suspect the presence of this oil sand from the air," said Cam in *Oilweek* (October 15, 1962). "You need to land and hit it with a hammer and section the outcrop."

The sandstone was found at two exposures 36 miles apart, and Cam estimated it to be as much as 80 feet thick, with recoverable reserves anywhere from 40 to 60 million barrels of oil per square mile. For him, it easily rivaled the largest known oil deposit in the world at that time—the Athabasca oil sands in the Fort McMurray area of Alberta. Cam believed the oil sands could be produced using the same mining and separation methods proposed for the Athabasca sands; however, the location presented challenges. "If it were closer to civilization it would be as easy as Athabasca to produce—or possibly easier. Problem Number One naturally is transport and markets." He felt the sands were worth producing, but for him the true significance of the find was that it proved there were oil reservoirs in the Arctic Islands. "All we need is a good combination of reservoir and structure and they will probably produce flowing oil conditions."

The Marie Bay Oil Sands outcrop forms a ridge on Melville Island. Photo provided by Sproule Associates.

Serene Arctic waters reflect an iceberg sculpture in the Western Bylot area, Greenland. Photo provided by Sproule Associates.

The Greenarctic Consortium

Cam Sproule's venture into Greenland was a natural extension of his activities in the Arctic. The Greenarctic Consortium was a Danish-Canadian group established in February 1969 to conduct exploration for natural gas, petroleum, and mineral resources north of the ice cap (north of 74 degrees 30 minutes North Latitude)—about 50,000 square miles. The founding members were Ponderay Exploration Co. Ltd. (60 percent, Joe Milner, president and chairman), Dr. J.C. Sproule (10 percent, which was intended to end up as a J.C. Sproule and Associates asset), and Niels A. Anderson (30 percent). Greenex Minerals Ltd., of which Cam was president, was incorporated in March 1969, and was a member company of the Consortium.

Joe Milner negotiated the exploration rights with the Danish government, which was more than willing to have foreign investors. According to the Calgary Herald (October 8, 1970), it was predicted that copper, cobalt, zinc, and silver deposits could be mined to the tune of $100 million by 1975.

J.C. Sproule and Associates was the senior consultant for the exploration work, and John Stuart-Smith was the geological party chief in the first field season (1969). Like their other Arctic work, it was preceded by interpretation of aerial photographs. Most of the work involved mapping and photography of the terrain, and taking samples of rock deposits. According to field party member Wally Drew, work began at Station Nord, the Danish weather station in the northeast, and moved across the land to the northwest. Geophysical surveys and geological mapping continued in the early 1970s.

Upon Cam's death in May 1970, Cam's wife, Maude, became president of Greenex Minerals. Almost a year later, in March 1971, Cam's 10 percent interest was transferred to Greenex. By December 1971, Ponderay Exploration and Greenex Minerals had amalgamated to form Greenland Exploration Company Ltd., to manage the Greenarctic Consortium.

The Greenarctic Consortium submitted a proposal to the Danish government in June 1973 to do further exploration and development in Greenland, including drilling of three wells. But it was rejected, primarily because new concession regulations were to be drawn up and legislated. The Consortium waited several years for these regulations, but they were not forthcoming.

In a letter sent in October 1973 to all members and directors of the Greenarctic Consortium, Milner proposed that all members and farmout partners sort out their interests in the venture, using acreage earned as a percentage of the total, so that interests might be sold to those willing to continue to contribute capital to the effort:

In my view, the Consortium has become an unwieldy vehicle through which to conduct the exploration in Greenland principally because of the division of interests which has arisen out of the various farmout blocks. Additionally, it is quite clear that most of the present partners are either unwilling or unable to continue to fund the activities of the Consortium.

In early 1974, the Consortium interests were pooled, and a new company—Greenarctic Consortium Ltd.—was formed; Greenex Minerals (the Sproule estate) held a 27.91 percent interest. Milner was optimistic that this change, along with obtaining additional (especially European) partners, would improve their chances of obtaining drilling rights. By that time, the Consortium had been active in Greenland for six years and had spent close to $3 million.

Three years later, Greenland Exploration's annual report, dated February 1977, indicated that the Greenland exploration and development project was a bust. There were still no development permits in effect and the investment was being "written down." The Consortium began selling its assets, including geological data obtained in Greenland.

Sproule's Greenland camp steels itself for ice fog. Photo provided by Sproule Associates.

Winter Harbour

In 1961, Dome Petroleum of Calgary, under President Jack Gallagher, drilled the first well in Canada's Arctic Islands. Situated at Winter Harbour, on the southern shore of Melville Island, it was the northernmost well in the world at that time. The selection of the Winter Harbour anticline for drilling was based on GSC data and aerial photography, and confirmed by surface mapping. The cost of the well was borne by 13 different oil companies and mining groups who held petroleum and natural gas permits in the Arctic Islands.

The target was the Allen Bay reef (about 450 million years old), and the primary objective was to evaluate all prospective oil and gas sediments encountered to 10,000 feet. The drilling contract went to Peter Bawden Drilling of Calgary, which designated its Rig #22 for the job. Said Alan Bryant, Dome geologist at the time:

The rig was dismantled at the Simonette field, near Valleyview, Alberta and trucked to Edmonton where it was completely overhauled before being loaded onto 20 rail cars and moved by rail to Montreal. There, at the docks, it joined the other supplies: two D-7 cats, a Nodwell tracked vehicle, a 10-ton Hayes truck, nine cargo sleds, 4,400 drums of diesel fuel, 232 drums of aviation fuel, 111 drums of lubricating oil, 500 pallets of drilling mud and cement, a complete ATCO pre-fabricated camp, 20 tons of food, and innumerable other items to keep the rig operating and 25 men comfortable for three months or more.

The materials were to be delivered by the M.V. Thora Dan, a Danish ship reinforced for ice-breaking. It left Montreal on August 1, 1961, and after being held up in Resolute Bay for several days because of ice, dropped anchor in Winter Harbour on August 20. Unloading was completed on the 30th, and in the next 11 days, the rig was moved to the drill site—just over a kilometre away—the camp was assembled, and a landing strip prepared. The well was spudded on September 10. The weather was a significant factor in the drilling operations:

The actual temperatures were not much different from those encountered on the northern mainland of Canada, but combined with the higher humidities at this maritime location, and higher wind velocities, the discomfort and danger for outside workers was much increased. The wind chill was reduced somewhat by enclosing the sides of the drilling floor and the lower part of the derrick with sheets of plywood, but the very nature of the drilling operation prevented the total enclosure of the work area. The worst conditions were encountered between the 24th of December and the 25th of January. During this period almost 115 hours (4.75 days) of rig time were lost, predominantly due to low temperatures combined with high winds, often greater than 40 mph, preventing tripping to change drilling bits. On the 31st of December and 1st of January winds gusted at 80 to 100 mph with temperatures of -24°F, while on the 23rd and 24th of January, temperatures dropped to -58°F with winds to 20 mph. On this occasion, the blocks and crown sheaves at the top of the derrick froze solid while the drillpipe was out of the hole, resulting in a 32-hour delay.

In early December, the well reached its contract depth of 10,000 feet without revealing any major indications of oil or gas. Some porosity was seen in the Devonian sandstones during the first 2,000 feet, but the Devonian section was thicker than anticipated, so the Silurian beds were not encountered until 9,700 feet. Calcerous mudstone—the shaley equivalent of the porous dolomites and limestones—were encountered in the next 300 feet, and the decision to drill an additional 2,500 feet was made December 1. At 11,600 feet the anticipated dolomites were encountered, but proved to have very little porosity. Logs and wireline tests below 12,000 feet held little promise and abandonment plugs were run from the bottom, at 12,543 feet up to 2,385 feet. A small gas flow was detected between 2,385 and 1,048 feet, but operations at Winter Harbour terminated on the 7th of April, 1962, seven months from spudding.

"Though the well was not a commercial success," said Bryant, "it did prove the feasibility of transporting a rig to the Arctic Islands and drilling through an Arctic winter. And it did indicate the presence, small though it was, of subsurface hydrocarbons."

A seismic survey later showed that the well just missed the leading edge of the fault-repeated Thumb Mountain section and found the porous and water-bearing section in the lower slice. The first gas show in the Arctic Islands was recorded from the lower part of the Devonian sand facies on this structure.

Gordon Jones attempted to group together all the companies in the oil sands area, in order to pool the land, but met with little success. Nevertheless, going through the process gave him valuable experience upon which he would draw for the Panarctic Oils venture.

A subsequent study showed the Triassic sandstone oil-stained exposures to be spotty, thus downgrading the 40-million-barrel-per-square-mile estimate to a level that may not have been economic.

Sproule geologists completed assignments of varying magnitude in many parts of the region in the 1960s, even into Greenland. Ground checking, stratigraphic sampling, palaeontological work, geochemistry, and limited gravity and other geophysical studies were carried out fairly extensively, by Sproule and by others. Texaco, Elf, and Mobil, for example, were active during that time, as was the GSC. Cam's enthusiasm over the potential of hydrocarbon and metal discoveries in the Arctic Islands never faded. His determination that these resources be developed led him to the consortium concept, and eventually Panarctic Oils.

The first deep-well drilling was at Winter Harbour on Melville Island in 1961. Other wells, by Round Valley Oil at Resolute Bay and by Domex on Bathurst Island, were drilled two years later, but further drilling was delayed until 1969. Substantial accumulations of hydrocarbons had not been found in the first three wells. Cam Sproule thought the site of the Winter Harbour well was badly chosen, but nevertheless preferred to look on the bright side when it came to all three wells. "Valuable experience and information has been gained," he said in the 1964 CIM *Bulletin* article (although he pointed out in a January 1968 presentation to the Canadian Institute of Surveying that the holes had not added substantially to knowledge of the well-exposed *geology* of the area). He suggested only that expansion and refinement of preliminary exploration methods would limit the drilling of exploratory dry holes in the future:

> In order to improve the ratio between potentially productive wells and dry holes in Arctic oil and gas exploration, it will be necessary to set the stage by promoting the following conditions:
>
> (a) Further detailed geological and related geophysical studies must be carried out.
>
> (b) There must be cooperation among operators and landholders.
>
> (c) Management, professional, and technical personnel must be provided with a realistic background of Arctic conditions.

A New Plan Emerges

In 1964 and 1965, Arctic Islands exploration began to decline. Small Canadian companies with permits lacked the funds to pursue the more expensive phases of exploration, and plays were being developed elsewhere, where returns on investment were faster. Land holdings dropped to 41 million acres from the previous peak of 63 million, according to *The Oil and Gas Journal* (July 25, 1966). It became desirable to pool the resources of the diverse entities, so that exploration in this remote, expensive area could proceed in a more sustained and effective manner. The end result was the formation of Panartic Oils.

Early in 1967, *offshore* Arctic exploration was begun by Global Marine, a Sproule client that had drilled Canada's first offshore wells, and many others followed in the next 18 months in the excitement following the launch of Panarctic Oils (including Panarctic itself) and the revelation of the Prudhoe Bay discovery in Alaska. This offshore work was an important impetus for greater attention to environmental concerns, and considerable research in that regard was subsequently undertaken.

The consensus of opinion today appears to be that thorough development of resources in the Arctic Islands will wait for shortages in more economic areas of the world. Cam Sproule's vision for Arctic development thus persists, though its realization progresses at a pace that would have undoubtedly frustrated him.

Test drilling is undertaken on the south side of Barrow Dome, Sabine Peninsula, Melville Island. Photo provided by Lois Harding.

In June 1971, just a year after Cam's death, then Minister of Indian Affairs and Northern Development Jean Chretien (current Prime Minister of Canada) honoured Cam Sproule's memory and his considerable contribution to Arctic exploration and resource development. He initiated the naming after Cam of a northwestern peninsula on Melville Island, a 16,000-acre jut of land about 600 miles inside the Arctic Circle. The Sproule company had discovered the oil sands on the peninsula, and the first two wells drilled by Panarctic Oils were drilled on the Island. The first deep well in the Arctic Islands (Winter Harbour) had been drilled there as well. A ceremony was held at Calgary's Petroleum Club, where Chretien presented Maude Sproule with a map highlighting Sproule Peninsula. "As long as there are maps of Canada," said Chretien, "Cam Sproule's name will be inscribed as a tribute to his development of Canada's North."

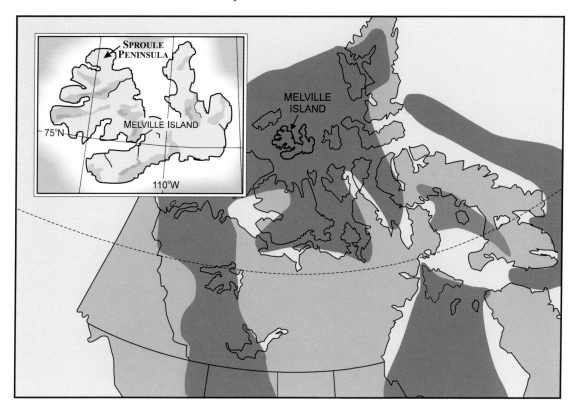

The Sproule Peninsula.

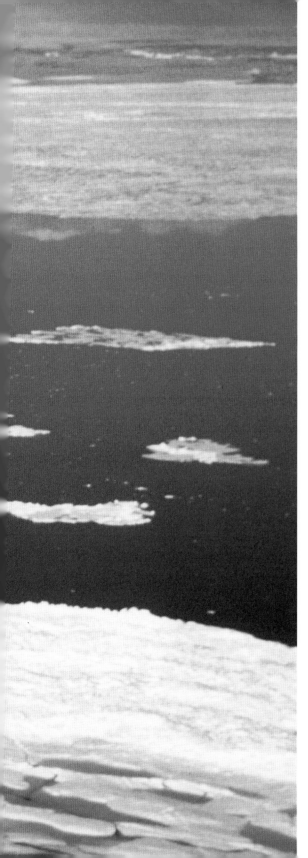

BOARDROOM TO BLOWOUT

FIGHTING FOR PANARCTIC OILS LTD.

The development of the North can only be carried out by men who are prepared to lose everything when they gamble, or to win riches beyond their dreams.

Cam Sproule

The jagged cliffs of Cape Majendie rise above Arctic waters off Grinnell Peninsula, Devon Island. Photo provided by Sproule Associates.

Birth of an Idea

In 1963, shortly after the well drilled on Bathurst Island came up dry, oil and gas plays in the North Sea, the Gulf Coast, and offshore California lured interest away from Canada's Arctic. According to Park Sullivan (with the Department of Indian Affairs and Northern Development starting in 1968), oil production in 1965 and 1966 in Canada was being pro-rated at rates well below maximum efficiency, and natural gas pipelines were full. Provincial oil and gas rights were fairly tightly held by major integrated American and Canadian companies. Companies were focusing their efforts in the oil-prone areas, postponing efforts in Canada's more remote areas until the world markets demanded new oil sources. The Rainbow oil field was discovered in northwestern Alberta in January 1965, and everybody rushed to get a piece of it.

This was the industry climate in the years that Cam Sproule was trying to keep things going in the Arctic Islands. In 1963, the first permits issued for the Islands were due, and some of the holders of those permits were letting them go. These small, independent companies and individuals were having difficulty financing their expensive Arctic exploration projects and could see more immediate rewards elsewhere. Gordon Jones said:

> We had many clients who were coming to us and saying, "We're having a real problem finding the money to keep exploring. If you hear of somebody that has got some money to spend on our lands, we would be very interested." We had put up a great deal of our own money, not to mention our clients' money—a great deal for a relatively small consulting company—because we assumed we would reap the benefits of that investment later on. We were beginning to realize that things weren't developing as fast as we originally anticipated and that there were other discoveries competing with the Arctic Islands.

It became clear to Cam, and many others, that Arctic exploration and development could only survive if those involved joined forces, sharing both the expenses and the rewards. Cam had already convinced his clients to share regional geological

Glacial drift dams a lake on Axel Heiberg Island. Photo provided by Sproule Associates.

92

information in the Islands. According to Sullivan, J. C. Sproule and Associates organized a series of syndicated exploration programs whereby rights holders could purchase geophysical and geological surveys that could meet the work requirements of their exploration permits. "These programs were effectively fostered under a provision in the regulations granting the Chief of Oil and Gas the discretionary power to consider work done outside the permit area as work evaluating the oil and gas potential under the permit itself. This greatly facilitated Arctic exploration." Rapidly rising costs of exploration programs demanded that those costs be shared by the individual holders. The syndicated programs were the answer for many of the smaller firms. It was an evolution of that process that led to Panarctic Oils.

Sproule (Gordon Jones in particular) had also tried to amalgamate the holdings of the various companies with permits in the area of the oil sand discovery on Melville Island, so they were prepared for what they might face in such a venture. Said Gordon:

> We grouped together all the companies in the general area into an agreement that would pool the land. That particular plan really didn't go ahead very far, because at that time oil sands were not commercial in the Arctic Islands. It did get the idea of land pooling going, and we learned some of the techniques to do it.

In December 1964, Cam was talking with a client, Eric Connelly of Pembina Pipelines, who had acquired Arctic Island permits in 1962 with the idea that control of the lands from which oil would be produced would put Pembina in a better position to develop the pipeline. Cam mentioned casually to Connelly that all he needed was $30 million to complete the exploration phase in a systematic fashion, covering all of the land permits as a group, instead of in pieces. It was clear to him that a workable project could be developed, provided there was control over the dominant portion of the lands in the basin by a single operator: the basin area could be operated as though it was a concession, thus enabling the operator to study the complete basin prospects and then select those areas for drilling that were most likely to produce oil. Connelly liked the idea and thought the financing might be possible. Gordon said Cam rushed into his office, and they immediately got out some maps to look at potential well sites and determine what work could be done. "We rather quickly fleshed out a program. Doc Sproule immediately sent out a bunch of two-page letters to clients to show them how they would benefit from exploration in their permit area; that is, how it would upgrade their land."

They were off and running.

The Proposal

Initially, Cam Sproule and Eric Connelly planned a joint venture. Their idea was to sell shares in a new company, Panarctic Oils, which would then invest in exploration of land that permittees had farmed out to them. Great Circle Petroleum was also created, in the spring of 1965, to manage the shareholding of Canadians not in the oil business but wanting to take part.

In June 1965, Cam put together a preliminary proposal and budget for a five-year exploration program in the Islands. He argued, as he had argued since setting foot on the Islands, that problems with markets and transportation were minor considering the potential oil reserves—33.2 billion barrels, which he considered a conservative estimate. He touted Western Europe, the British Isles, and Montreal as the principal markets for the oil, and reiterated arguments for pipelines and open-air storage tanks within the Islands, and submarine tankers and ships supported by ice-breakers to take the oil to market. He cited Petropar's interests in the Islands as evidence that the economics of development were feasible: "The fact that Petropar (a 51 percent French Government-owned company) is spending large sums of money on the Islands and is the largest single operator there, bears witness to their own views on the economics of Arctic Islands potential oil production."

After six years studying the Islands' geology, Cam was confident he could pinpoint the areas most likely to contain oil or gas accumulation. He believed the five-year exploratory program would verify subsurface features identified by surface work, and uncover further leads. He identified 11 such areas and trends, with the largest groups of wells planned for northwestern Melville Island, in the area of the Marie Bay oil sands. He proposed a program that first involved geological exploration, followed by geophysical exploration, and then exploration drilling, beginning

Gordon Jones and Cam pore over Arctic acreage. Photo provided by the Sproule family.

94

in the western areas and proceeding eastward. He planned shallow (3,500-foot), intermediate (6,500-foot), and deep (12,000–15,000-foot) wells, initially with one shallow-hole rig, one medium-hole rig, and two deep-hole rigs. The only wells drilled in the Arctic Islands up to this point were the three that had come up dry—on Melville, Bathurst, and Cornwallis Islands. But Cam dismissed these, saying that the necessity of drilling dry holes of this type could be avoided with "prudent preliminary geological and geophysical studies." According to Charlie Bulmer, Cam maintained that the three wells had been drilled in locations chosen for their accessibility, rather than their geological merit, to meet exploratory expenditure requirements of the permits.

Cam also argued for a sustained 12-months-a-year drilling program on the Islands:

> The cost of drilling a single hole on the islands is excessive and is in the same general class as for a very deep hole in the mountains or foothills of northeastern British Columbia or the mainland of the Northwest Territories. That is because a great deal of the cost is due to transportation of equipment and supplies to and from inaccessible areas. If, however, the drilling program can be carried out over a considerable period, the resultant cost on a per hole basis is greatly reduced.

> It should also be pointed out that, when the program enters the exploitation stage, the drilling costs should be drastically reduced because of the available local supply of fuel to power the drilling rigs.

Getting it Out

In 1966, a scheme for a pipeline from the Islands was informally proposed by Panarctic Oils in a report outlining their exploration and drilling program for Great Circle Petroleum:

> It would seem apparent at this time that the use of pipelines from the Islands to the open Atlantic water is most economical.

> If it is assumed that oil is found on Melville Island in quantities capable of production at 300,000 barrels per day, and that this production is to be moved to the Montreal market area, the following transportation system could be built with minor extensions of existing technology:

> The system would comprise a pipeline 500 miles long, extending from Melville Island to Makinson Inlet on the east coast of Ellesmere Island via Byam Martin Island, Bathurst Island, Devon Island, North Kent Island and Ellesmere; and open surface storage reservoir and tanker loading facility near the head of Makinson Inlet; and an open surface storage reservoir and tanker loading facility near Godthaab, Disko Island off the west coast of Greenland. The overland portions of the pipeline would consist of a single 36" diameter insulated pipe supported above ground on piling extending through the active layer into permanently frozen material. The submarine portions of the pipeline would consist of multiple lines of smaller diameter pipe (e.g. five 16" pipes) laid on the ocean floor at sufficient depth to escape the grounding of icebergs. The transition sections from overland to submarine pipelines would be ditched and buried for a sufficient distance offshore to escape the effects of "fast ice" movement on the shoreline.

> The pipeline would be operated on a year-round basis, and would deliver oil to tankers at Makinson Inlet (during the six months of navigability available to this point with minimal ice-breaker assistance) for shipment. During this same six months navigation season tankers would operate on a shuttle basis to transfer the winter accumulation of oil in the open surface reservoir near Makinson Inlet to a similar reservoir near Godthaab. Since Godthaab is open for navigation on a year-round basis, a source for winter deliveries of oil to market would thus be provided.

> It is estimated that the pipeline system and related storage loading and unloading facilities could be created with a total capital investment of 285 million dollars, and that a system tariff of $0.53 per barrel would produce a normal industry-level return on this investment. It is further estimated that a weighted average tanker tariff (including the effect of the seasonal employment of tankers on the Makinson Inlet–Godthaab shuttle) of $0.26 per barrel would apply to the transportation of the oil from Makinson to Montreal.

> If these transportation costs ($0.53 + $0.26 = $0.79/Bbl.) are subtracted from a crude oil price at Montreal of $2.80/Bbl., an amount of $2.01/Bbl. remains for finding, lifting and gathering the crude oil.

The "bottom line" for the proposed exploration program was $30 million. Cam figured that oil discoveries made by the end of the first five years would allow the operation to move into the exploitation phase, and he estimated credits related to drilling would amount to almost twice the $30-million expenditure. He predicted that at least 20 oil discoveries would be made:

> If the above program is carried out it is our confirmed opinion that at least three out of five of the proposed deep holes would be productive and that, therefore, approximately 12 deep hole discoveries will be made. It also seems reasonable to assume that one out of four of the medium depth holes would be productive and that, therefore, two discoveries will be made, of the eight planned for drilling. We believe also that considering the nature of the prospects, one-half of the shallow test holes should be productive, which should account for six more discoveries.

Cam also anticipated gas discoveries, which he presumed would at first supply power to the oil and mining operations on the Islands.

In August 1965, Eric Connelly held discussions with A. Deane Nesbitt (of the investment firm Nesbitt, Thomson and Company Limited of Montreal) and key members of the federal government about how to raise the money. He also worked with Ross Tolmie, a friend and business associate who was accustomed to working with the government. On July 22, 1965, they met with Arthur Laing, then minister of Indian Affairs and Northern Development, who supported the plan and fought in the Cabinet for it, despite opposition. (Ultimately, Laing spoke personally to Prime Minister Lester Pearson, persuading him by using the issue of Arctic sovereignty.) Laing suggested Connelly and Sproule go and get the farmouts in place, as proof it could be done.

They proceeded to do just that; some of the farmout agreements that Cam negotiated even included drilling commitments in his eagerness to get some companies signed up. Gordon Jones became concerned that Cam had committed most of the money before they even had it. Said Digby Hunt, assistant deputy minister in Laing's department in 1971: "The trouble was that his enthusiasm ran away with his judgement. He said to me personally, and I'm not exaggerating, that he was sure the very first well we drilled would be a commercial oil well—a winner." A deadline of January 31, 1966 was set by the federal government to get the agreements in place.

Deane Nesbitt proposed a tax concession from the federal government to allow private investors to write off 50 percent of their risk expenditures. The concern was that those *not* in the oil business get tax concessions similar to those that *were* in the oil business. They met with Mitchell Sharp,

Ice caps endure on the sculpted peaks of southeastern Axel Heiberg Island. Photo provided by Sproule Associates.

then minister of Trade and Industry, in January 1966, but the government wasn't prepared to go along with the tax concession, especially given the Carter Commission study on taxation, which was to recommend withdrawal of depletion allowance benefits from oil and mining companies. Instead, the idea of a direct loan, equivalent to what the tax deduction would have meant, was put forward. A 50:50 industry–public investment split was suggested, and the Northern Minerals Exploration program was born. The deadline for completion of the farmout agreements was extended, and the details of the Northern Minerals Act were worked out.

In the end, the Northern Mineral Exploration program, announced September 6, 1966, allowed for up to 40 percent of the funds required for an approved exploration program—carried out in either Yukon or the Northwest Territories in search of minerals or oil—to be provided by the Department of Northern Affairs and National Resources. If the program was successful, the grant was repayable over a ten-year period, commencing when production started; if unsuccessful, the grant would be regarded as a contribution to the northern exploration effort and was not repayable. So when the dust settled, the federal government had agreed to a forgivable loan to the Panarctic Oils exploration program of $6 million. Nesbitt agreed to finance Great Circle Petroleum, which represented the public interests (including the government loan) to the tune of $15 million if Panarctic Oils came up with the other $15 million from industry.

Panarctic Oils Ltd.

Cam Sproule and Eric Connelly incorporated Panarctic Oils on May 27, 1966 so that the farmout agreements could be registered properly. In the *Calgary Herald* (May 31, 1966), Jim Armstrong wrote that the reported incorporation of Panarctic, "is the best news Arctic development has received since federation." Connelly would be president and Cam the executive vice-president and general manager; Gordon Jones would be corporate secretary. Said Gordon:

> Sproule, I think, was really the leader in terms of ideas and money put in, but I think the financial community was a little scared of this "wild geologist." Eric Connelly was seen to be a more solid sort of businessman—a financial man—so that's why he became president instead of Sproule.

A 40 percent interest in Panarctic Oils would be held by participating companies, which would contribute cash and/or permit rights; 40 percent by Great Circle Petroleum; and 20 percent by J.C. Sproule and Associates. Armstrong praised Cam's efforts:

It will take a person like Dr. Sproule, outspoken and single-minded, to get such a project off the ground and running smoothly. He also has the ability to sustain interest in the north, for he projects an optimism very rare among professional geologists and engineers.

Cam was prepared to give up his consulting company and devote himself entirely to the new enterprise. "His own business suffered as he committed time, energy and a million dollars of his own money into what had become his personal dream," said Max Foran, in his presentation to the Western Studies Conference in 1983. Gordon estimated that Cam devoted 95 percent of his professional time over three years to the Panarctic project. Gordon was Sproule's chief agent in negotiating the land agreements. "It needed a lot of patience and diplomacy, and that was one thing Sproule wasn't strong on," he said. Ironically, Sproule clients saw that Panarctic would spend money on their behalf, and saw no point in spending their own, so J.C. Sproule and Associates' business suffered during this period.

Negotiations with numerous small companies required some time, and several postponements of permit obligations (the last to December 31, 1967) had to be obtained from the Department of Indian Affairs and Northern Development. The farmout agreements were complex and constantly changing. Each was different from the next, because each piece of land had to be valued individually. "That was quite tricky," said Gordon.

> Fortunately, because we did know more about the geology than anybody else in the industry at the time, we were able to persuade virtually all of our clients that, in fact, we did have a good basis for judgement. They trusted that we were treating everybody fairly, on an equal sort of basis, and this was a rather unique situation.

Only the best land prospects for discovery were sought, but others were also included if the agreement depended on it. All agreements also had to be legalized; in the end, 23 major agreements with 75 oil companies were hammered out.

Cam's chief negotiator, Gordon Jones. Photo provided by Gordon Jones.

Over two years had passed since the idea first came to light in December 1964, and no work by Panarctic Oils had yet been done. In March 1967, Cam was still trying to get the last $4 million from oil companies who had a stake in the Arctic Islands. It was an ongoing struggle, and the stress may have contributed to a serious illness he suffered that winter.

The Hurdles

There were probably many reasons why industry players were hesitant: potential investors were undoubtedly deterred by the Carter Commission, the long-term risk involved, and the disinterest of the majors. To hold permits, companies either had to put out exploration funds or allow the permits to revert to the Crown, and it appeared that some of the majors were waiting in the wings to pick up the permits at bargain prices. The majors also may not have welcomed another government oil company, and government regulations in the Arctic favoured Canadian companies. Wrote Earle Gray in *Oilweek* (December 18, 1967):

> The foreign-controlled majors certainly weren't barred, but they may have decided they didn't want to compete in an area where government favors—such as exploration loans repayable only in the event commercial production is established—were reserved for Canadian-controlled interests.

There were plenty of good places around the world for the majors to invest, and in Canada many of the majors were heavily committed to offshore exploration. In addition, no company was allowed to hold more than 10 percent interest in Panarctic Oils, and this restriction may have discouraged some major companies from joining the project.

The federal government feared the majors would "deep-freeze" the program (this had already happened in the Northwest Territories), leaving French-controlled Petropar Canada as the most active company in the area. As Pat Carney (later Minister of Energy, Mines, and Resources) wrote in 1968: "Ottawa wasn't anxious to have de Gaulle [*the President of France, who spoke out in favour of Quebec sovereignty*] stake out a position in the arctic." But Cam was prepared to go to foreign investors if he couldn't muster the support he needed from Canadian companies. As an avid nationalist, he had worked very hard to keep Panarctic Canadian, despite American companies eager to invest. Interestingly, Petropar participated in the Panarctic venture (it farmed out four million acres to the company), and was prepared to gear its own exploration program to complement the efforts of the joint group. British Petroleum also farmed out some land interests to Panarctic.

The Arctic sun shines on snow-swept mountains in the Otto Fiord area of Ellesmere Island. Photo provided by Sproule Associates.

Cam came close to his objectives several times, but commitments came and went while everyone was waiting for things to be finalized. "Sproule used to say it was like trying to pick up a bunch of snakes," said Gordon Jones. "While you are leaning down to pick up two, two others slip away." By May 1967, the money had still not been raised, and the deadline for the farmout options (June 30, 1967) was rapidly approaching. (The permittees were required to have six months to make arrangements to meet their work obligations before the deadline of December 31, 1967.)

The New Deal

A hint of revising the program was published in the *Daily Oil Bulletin* (May 16, 1967): a suggestion had been made to reduce the program to three years, at a cost of $20 million, with an additional $10 million raised during the three years to finance the following two years. This would also reduce Panarctic's initial exploration funds by two-thirds, at least for the first three years. With current investor support for the $20 million plan, Cam was confident he could raise the money by the deadline.

But it was not to be.

It became apparent that, even with the new program, it would take too long to come up with the money. On the July 1st weekend 1967, everything came to a head. "We realized that something had to be done very quickly or the whole lot would collapse," said Gordon Jones. "In fact, many people were predicting that it *would* collapse." Cam and Gordon met with their lawyers and John Taylor of Canadian Pacific Oil and Gas Company (CPOG), Bob Armstrong of Cominco, and Jack Gallagher of Dome. They spent the long weekend trying to work out the solution: they approached the federal government regarding equity financing. A new deal was struck and the 75 companies involved were approached for their approval. Everything was legalized in about three weeks—and it was big news: 20 companies had put up $11 million and the Government of Canada was its biggest shareholder—in for $9 million. Bruce Phillips, of the *Calgary Herald's* Ottawa bureau, wrote (December 14, 1967):

> Nothing quite like the partnership between the federal government and 20 private companies for Arctic oil exploration has ever been tried before in this country. But on the face of it, formation of Panarctic Oils Limited with the government as a 45 per cent shareholder is so logical the only question it raises is why it hasn't been tried before.

Jim Armstrong was less optimistic. In *Canadian Petroleum* (February 1968) he wrote:

Compared to most exploration budgets in virgin country, the $20 million (or $30 million, depending likely on the results of the first investments) is peanuts. Sums equal to this, or more, have already been sunk in Canada's offshore waters without results. And on the Northwest Territories mainland, where, as an example, a single company spent $1 million per hole on a 10-well drilling program, and then dropped the land. A number of majors have been active on the mainland for years without big results, though they feel sure that eventually a major strike will be made.

Arthur Laing made the announcement in the House of Commons on December 12, 1967. The federal government would put up $9,022,500 and 20 private companies would put up $11,027,500. It was an investment, not a loan under the Northern Minerals Exploration program (though it would be handled under the terms of the program). In return for 45 percent of the exploration costs, the government would hold 45 percent of the common shares and 45 percent of the preference shares Panarctic would issue. Considerable continued expenditure was anticipated if the exploration program was sufficiently successful, with the government perhaps taking a reduced interest, making way for increased private or public participation in the future.

Seventy-five companies were to see their interests explored under Canadian auspices. In his announcement to the House of Commons, Laing said:

Without Panarctic many of these interests might have been lost to their Canadian owners because of their inability to finance exploration.

Mr. Speaker it is gratifying to tell the House that this great Canadian resource potential will be assessed by Canadians and that majority ownership will rest with Canadians. This is a unique project. It brings together a large number of interests in the private sector on the one hand and the Government on the other, under one organization capable of effecting the economies so necessary in the North. Here we have a new development approach in this special region of the country with optimistic prospects for building the economy of our northern lands.

About 15 million of the 44 million acres in the Panarctic Oils deal would likely have been given up because of a lack of funds to meet work commitments, and it was generally believed that large international companies would have picked up the acreage and held it for many years, doing only the minimum work necessary. As it turned out, private participation in Panarctic was 56 percent Canadian; combined with the government's share it was 76 percent Canadian-owned. As long as the government interest remained above 10 percent, no further stock in the company could be issued, and none could be transferred without their approval. The government was thus able to ensure Canadian control of Panarctic. If the full $30 million program was completed, the non-resident interest in the lands would be less than 20 percent.

Laing had always believed that it was in the public's interest to know what mineral resources the north possessed, that ownership and control of development should remain in Canadian hands, and that the Canadian people should be the immediate and direct beneficiaries of any profitable exploitation of the area. In an article entitled *Arctic Search* printed in the *Calgary Herald* (December 13, 1967), it was written:

> The willingness of Ottawa to invest has meant the difference between the scheme being able to go ahead now or being delayed for many more years.
>
> A shortage of risk capital has long been one of the hard facts of Canada's economic life.
>
> The result has too often been that development of primary wealth-producing resources has been delayed, to the general loss of the national economy, or foreign capital has been encouraged to take on the job.
>
> The trouble with the latter eventuality is that it has excluded Canadians to a large measure from sharing to the fullest extent in the development of their own natural resources.

One advantage of government participation was that, if it succeeded, a Canadian company would control Canada's major oil region, and a pattern for northern development would be set. (In 1968, 70 percent of the Canadian oil industry was owned by the United States.) It would also make Canada a truly significant player in world oil production, able to provide the Western Hemisphere with its lowest-cost reserves. Canada would join the ranks of such countries as England and France, whose

Lionel Singleton takes time out at the Isachsen Formation on Ellef Ringnes Island.
Photo provided by Sproule Associates.

governments had invested in the oil business. With government support, not only would Panarctic get off the ground, but development in transportation technology would also be stimulated. The production of oil and gas in the Islands would also provide support for the exploration for metallic minerals, both in the Islands and on the mainland.

Setting Up

The largest single private stake was held by two subsidiaries of Canadian Pacific Investments— Cominco and CPOG—which put up more than $3.6 million each for more than an 18 percent total interest. This was rather ironic, given Cam's "run-in" with the Canadian Pacific Railway (who owned Canadian Pacific Investments) over the location of a right-of-way in front of his Fourth Avenue office. The *Daily Oil Bulletin* (May 16, 1967) recognized the importance of CPR's early commitment to the project:

> It seems worthy of note at this point that it was the C.P.R. that pioneered the trans-continental railway nearly 100 years ago. The fact that the C.P.R. group is now in the forefront of an attempt to pioneer the development of Canada's last Frontier, the Arctic Islands area, is a strong commentary on the progressive attitude of a healthy private enterprise with profits available for expenditure and prepared to place them, along with those of Canadian private citizens, on the much-needed development of a new area that might otherwise not be developed for many years to come.

The next largest interest (5.4 percent) was held by the Dome companies. Nineteen Canadian oil companies took part, along with one American company (Bocadel Oil Corporation of Texas). The stakes were estimated at 50 to 60 billion barrels of oil and 200 to 300 trillion cubic feet of natural gas, plus metallic minerals. Almost half of the private participation was by mining interests. Interestingly, Ed Tovell, with Dome at the time, said that part of the problem in raising money was that Cam was pursuing numerous mining companies, who weren't accustomed to spending much money on exploration.

> Mining companies really did not know the oil business, and a budget of $300,000 to a mining company for exploration is a lot of money. To an oil company that's just a drop in the bucket— that's only one seismic crew for a month. Really, the two didn't meld, and so Cam was always working against himself trying to find money.

But in *Oilweek* (January 8, 1968) Cam said, "Without this, we would never have raised the money. For some of the participants, the metallic prospects may be as important as the oil; for others, it was the icing on the cake."

Ultimately, Dome Petroleum was considered the best choice for operating the new company, because Panarctic would be moving into geophysics and drilling, and Dome had both the capabilities and the experience, especially in the Arctic (Dome had drilled the first well in the Islands, at Winter Harbour on Melville Island).

Although Cam thought he and his company were the best choice for operations, their experience was with exploration geology and economic evaluations. Even so, Cam was to express his opinion rather vehemently through letters over the years for which Dome held the operations contract (initially to December of 1968, but ultimately to the end of 1970), as evidenced in a letter to a colleague dated December 2, 1969:

> I hesitate to recommend that you get involved with Panarctic at this time, inasmuch as it is being operated by a gang of "Nincompoops", who should know enough to turn the operation over to experts, but they do not seem to know that. If a strong man would come along and say that he would take it over providing he had no interference from said "Nincompoops", then all would be rosy.

Jack Gallagher, former president of Dome, said he hadn't wanted the Panarctic operation because the company had less than a five percent interest, and was short-handed for their own operations. The credits Dome had acquired from the Winter Harbour drilling would carry them well into the 1970s. But pressure came from Dome Mines, who had a 20 percent share of Dome Petroleum, as well as other mining companies. John MacDonald, senior assistant deputy minister of Indian Affairs and Northern Development, also exerted pressure for Dome to take the job on. Said Gallagher:

> Unfortunately, and understandably, Cam Sproule was badly hurt by not becoming the operator of his baby, Panarctic. I know that he felt that I'd taken the operation away from him, which couldn't be further from the truth. Operating Panarctic caused Dome a great disruption and distraction of our limited top personnel in a relatively small company, and we feel that Panarctic indirectly cost Dome untold dollars in our exploration and operation in Western Canada.

Mesozoic beds meet icy waters on Ellesmere Island. Photo provided by Sproule Associates.

Ed Tovell, who attended the "11th-hour" meetings, remembers things happening a little differently, saying that Gallagher and he decided they would go along *only* if they could operate the company. Nevertheless, Gallagher recognized Cam's contribution in an article published in *Oilweek* (December 18, 1967): "He was the author of the idea, and he did a great job of visualizing the project. The accolades belong to him."

The federal government wasn't interested in the management and operation of the program and provided only one government representative—John MacDonald—to the 14-man Board of Directors. Pat Carney quoted MacDonald on Panarctic's search for oil in the Arctic Islands: "It is still a gamble. But even if we fail, we will have done the right thing.... If we are going to occupy the north, we must do more than send RCMP boats through waving flags." Laing had said in his speech to the House of Commons: "There is no certainty that oil will be found. But no oil will be found unless exploration is carried out. This announcement signals the beginning of search, not certain success." (It was also pointed out that the money amounted to just 3/100ths of one percent of the federal budget.)

In his press release of December 12, 1967 Carl Nickle (editor of the *Daily Oil Bulletin* and a Panarctic investor) wrote:

> Private capital is undertaking a "four element gamble" without any guarantee: First, that mineral resources big enough to justify high cost of exploitation can be found; Second, that transport systems can be devised that would make Arctic Resources competitive in Canadian and Overseas markets; Third, that man can successfully challenge Northern elements, and in large numbers live and work in the Arctic; and Fourth, that the present and future Canadian governments will maintain resource and taxation policies favourable to risking of capital.

> The Arctic gamble reflects a confidence in the soundness of Canada, and of Canadians, and the belief that the significant program of exploration now starting will, during the decade of the 1970s, start fulfilling the hopes of the pioneer venturers of today.

John Taylor, general manager of CPOG, was named president (because his company held the largest share); Bob Armstrong, vice-president of exploration for Cominco, was named executive vice-president; and John Godfrey, land manager of Dome Petroleum, was named vice-president (the three companies—CPOG, Cominco, and Dome—were referred to as the "CPOG group"). There were 14 members on the Board of Directors of Panarctic. Any company with a five percent interest in Panarctic could have a director on the board. Companies with smaller interests could pool their interests and elect a director to represent them. (Cam Sproule served that function for Thor Exploration Company (sister corporation to Ranvik Oils), established to provide initial financing to Panarctic Oils.)

Even after putting the "new deal" together, major oil company participation remained light—according to *Oilgram* (January 19, 1968), British Petroleum, Chevron Standard, Burmah Oil, and Petropar Canada had small interests. W.O. Twaits, then Imperial Oil president said: "The reason we are not in the Arctic Islands is very simple. We just cannot see any economic way to get the oil out if you find any. It is a matter of limitations on the size of transport." John Godfrey wasn't worried about

The Panarctic tour group prepares for Arctic adventure, August 1968. The photo was sent to Cam by Jean Chretien, who stands at the bottom of the stairs (11th from the right). Cam is at the top of the stairs, just in front of the doorway. Photo provided by the Sproule family.

transporting the oil. "If we find oil in sufficient quantities, we'll move it." Other majors were concentrating their efforts on areas more easily produced than the Arctic Islands. After the Prudhoe Bay discovery offshore Alaska's North Slope in the summer of 1968, some may have regretted that decision. With the Arctic Islands lying roughly within the same geographical area as the Alaska find, the area became extremely attractive, and a speculative rush to file permits throughout the Mackenzie Delta resulted from the Prudhoe Bay find.

Earle Gray, in his editorial in *Oilweek* (December 18, 1967) expressed more concerns about markets. "It may be significant that not one of the 20 firms putting up the $11 million equity in Panarctic own a single refinery or marketing operation." He said that existing refiner-marketers were integrated operations, and thus would not be eager to buy oil from someone else when they had their own reserves to produce and sell. He suggested Panarctic get into the refining-marketing business: "Many large oil companies became integrated simply out of the necessity of establishing a market for their oil." No integrated companies were involved in the Panarctic deal.

The Fallout

In a letter to Cam dated December 22, 1967, John MacDonald wrote:

I think I am more proud of this venture than anything I have done in the public service. You can claim additional credit because if it had not been for the confidence we felt in you and the validity of your ideas, we would never have invested the effort we did to bring about the government participation. All in all it has been a most satisfying experience and I hope you feel as pleased as I do.

I certainly look forward to continued association with you. You must have been struck, as I was, at the remarkable spirit which moved such a widely diverse group of people as has been brought together in this effort. I think that too is a tribute to the strength of your idea.

James L. Buckley, in a letter dated December 21, 1967, also offered his congratulations:

This is just a note to express my admiration at the remarkable job which you and your associates have done in conceiving and finally launching the complex Panarctic enterprise. The vision was brilliant and the tenacity demonstrated during four years of frustrating difficulties was truly impressive.

I only hope that in addition to the deep feeling of personal satisfaction which you must now feel, you will have received a material recognition and personal stake in the results of the enterprise commensurate with your enormous contributions in the form of imagination, time, and personal risk which you have contributed to it.

But acknowledgement of his contribution was all Cam received. On August 30, 1967, an agreement had essentially been reached with Cam that the CPOG group would take over control of Panarctic Oils. The major players in the consortium had been nervous for some time about Cam heading up the large, highly complex, and politically sensitive company. They recognized that he was the best Arctic geologist there was, but as a businessman lacked experience with an operation of this magnitude. Jack Gallagher had expressed concern as early as May of that year about Cam's health and financial situation, and had called for a new general manager at that time. Digby Hunt recalled John MacDonald saying: "It is typical of many people who have the enthusiasm, the drive and the know-how to put something together, but once it is put together they may not be the best people to run it."

MacDonald was very concerned, according to Digby Hunt, that Cam be justly rewarded for his efforts. In their final agreement, dated October 15, 1967, Panarctic granted to Cam and Eric Connelly collectively a 10 percent net carried interest on oil, gas, and other minerals (including metals) produced from lands in the Arctic Islands. The agreement would hold in perpetuity, in exchange for their shares and the control of Panarctic that their shares represented. Eight percent went to Sproule and two percent to Connelly. At the time, the 10 percent net carried interest had no significant market value (though it had an intrinsic value), because no exploration had taken place and Panarctic had not acquired interests in the lands. Sproule paid $6,000 to Panarctic for his eight percent, and Sproularctic Holdings Ltd. was formed in March 1969 as a vehicle to hold the shares. A portion of the trust units created (eight million of them, a million for each one percent net carried interest) would go to Cam's personal company—Sproule Projects Ltd.—and a portion to him personally, which was inherited by his family at his death. The remainder were transferred to a number of his associates in J.C. Sproule and Associates. (Petrofina purchased Connelly's two percent, through his company Arctic Islands Resources, in February 1972, for over $6 million. This figure may have been largely based on the value of net carried interest calculated by consultant R. Alan Rudkin, who estimated the potential future reserves and forecast prices based on marketing the oil beginning in 1980.)

On September 28, 1967, a cheque for $350,000 was made out to J.C. Sproule and Associates for the geological data, and rights to them, pertaining to the Arctic Islands. Legal fees of $80,000 were also paid (and Eric Connelly personally received $26,000 for his efforts). The materials were for the exclusive use of Panarctic to December 31, 1968 or beyond, as long as Sproule's services were retained by the company. They were retained until December 31, 1969. Sproule conducted or supervised all exploratory field geological and related photogeological and photogrammetric work undertaken by

Sheets of ice break away from the bow of an Arctic vessel. Photo provided by Sproule Associates.

111

Panarctic in the Arctic Islands. In fact most of Sproule's work in the late 1950s and early 1960s laid the foundation for later drilling. During the two-year exclusive period, Sproule could not provide any services relating to Arctic Islands geology to any other person, except if that person was not in some arrangement with Panarctic.

According to daughters Anne and Judy, their father was devastated at being shut out from the management of the company he had put so much of himself into, though he remained on the Exploration Committee. Nora Tettensor's impression at the time was that, "He was very, very hurt that he didn't get on the Board, and so was everybody in the office."

Jim Armstrong wrote in *Canadian Petroleum* (February 1968):

To many who are fully aware of the single-minded determination of this outstanding man in pushing through Panarctic, the omission of Dr. Sproule in the final scheme was a shock. If he had not had the determination to carry on through three very disappointing years attempting to bring together dozens of companies and raise the necessary capital, Panarctic would have been stillborn.

Max Foran wrote:

In terms of his own personal ambitions it is unfortunate that Cam Sproule did not figure more prominently in the operation and direction of the project he had worked so hard to bring to fruition.

His boundless zeal and penchant for volatile spontaneity sometimes worried those of more reasonable and systematic corporate temper.

Fellow geologists sometimes winced at his sweeping generalizations and lack of preciseness, particularly with respect to geological extrapolations. In that sense, he might not have been considered the ideal of an infant company so politically sensitive as Panarctic. John Campbell Sproule was, however, a visionary with a dream that transcended the boundaries of his time. It was this vision and crusading zeal buttressed by thoroughgoing field work which has made Sproule easily the most important figure in the Canadian search for oil in the high Arctic.

Eventually, Cam was to be shut out completely. On May 11, 1970, just ten days prior to his death, he wrote to John Taylor:

A rather unusual situation has arisen whereby I have, as a member of the Panarctic Exploration Committee, been invited to attend an Exploration Committee meeting to be held in Ottawa on

May 13th. I have learned indirectly, however, that a proposed amendment to previous agreements, to be retroactive to March 1, 1970, is being introduced to the Panarctic Directors' meeting on May 13th and that the amendment is designed for the sole purpose of removing me from the Exploration Committee. This would appear to mean that if I go to Ottawa, it is probable that I shall be told I am ineligible to attend the meeting. That being the case, and in view of the Board's attitude toward my services, I do not see that my appearance in Ottawa could serve any useful purpose at this time.

In explaining my absence from this meeting, I should like to make it clear that my interest in serving Panarctic is no less than it ever has been. Indeed, *my personal and economic interest in Panarctic is still greater than it is in my own consulting firm* [italics added]. If, therefore, the climate in respect to the acceptability of my advice should change, I shall be only too pleased to assist in any way possible.

Panarctic Oils Gets Started

The permits farmed out to Panarctic represented more than 60 percent of the 70 million acres held in the Islands. The agreements gave Panarctic the right to earn an interest in the 44 million acres, when the three-year program was completed, that ranged from 50 to 90 percent. The company had an option to increase this interest by expanding the exploration program to $30 million.

Under the farmout agreements, Panarctic was committed to drilling 17 wells. Nine deep tests, six wildcats of medium depth, and two shallow tests were suggested in the press release written by Carl Nickle, dated December 12, 1967. And to be successful, any oil strike had to be big.

The three-year exploration program got under way with a seismic survey in March of 1968, at Marie Bay on Melville Island. It was finished in September with the completion of 600 miles of seismograph lines, which would provide structural information needed to select the first drilling sites. Drilling plans for the first two exploratory tests, on Melville Island, were announced the following January, and drilling was slated to begin in March of 1969.

A seismic crew lays lines offshore Lougheed Island. Photo provided by Panarctic Oils.

A tanker barge delivered enough basic supplies for a year's drilling, including 480,000 gallons of fuel, drilling fluid materials, three trucks, one crane, five trailers, tractors, cement, lumber, and other supplies. It was the first time that a tug-and-barge operation had been used to supply the far northern islands. It was made possible because the barge was fitted with the Alexbow ice plow (and pushed by the tug). It was the first time the device was tested in Arctic waters, though it had been tested successfully in the Great Lakes. It easily penetrated ice up to four feet thick and also handled ice between five and six feet thick. Cam Sproule had brought inventor Scott Alexander to a Calgary meeting of farmors. "The Alexbow, or some further development of this principle, could make the centuries-old idea of a northwest passage a reality, and open the mineral resources of the Arctic to world markets," Cam said in *Oilweek* (January 8, 1968).

Earle Gray, writing for *Oilweek* (January 27, 1969) played the guarded optimist on the search for Arctic oil:

> It will result in disappointment, at least for the wild-eyed optimists, not because the program is destined for failure, but because ultimate success will involve an expensive, difficult and long-fought battle. Vast reserves may indeed be found, but by all odds it is far more likely to be the result of patient effort rather than instant success. Exploration, development, transportation, and marketing — all these hurdles will ultimately be cleared, but only after vast amounts of money and a good many years.

In the eight years previous to Panarctic, $8 million had been spent on exploration work in the Arctic. Panarctic would spend $7 million per year, and a third of the $20-million budget would be eaten up by transportation costs, including vehicles such as graders and loaders needed in the Islands.

Panarctic's ice volcano steams at Drake Point, Melville Island. The relief well is in the foreground. Photo provided by Panarctic Oils.

Panarctic's history of discovery in the Arctic Islands began in 1969 with the discovery of gas at Drake Point on Sabine Peninsula, Melville Island (the first well to be drilled since the infamous three dry wells). The wildcat blew out of control on July 12. "It blew wild," said Charles Hetherington, first full-time president of Panarctic starting January 1, 1971. "In addition to gas sands, some water sands opened up and the gas blew the water up in the air, and it froze of course, forming a great ice cone 250 feet high. It looked like a volcano with steaming gas coming out of the top."

A second well was drilled about 1,100 feet from the first. This second Drake Point well, drilled in 1970, confirmed the natural gas. It turned out to be one of the largest natural gas reservoirs in Canada. It was abandoned shortly after, because there was no immediate market for the gas, and then an attempt to control the wild well was undertaken, seven months after the blowout, by drilling from the top of the second well directionally to the bottom of the wild one. This was not successful, so a well was spudded just 100 yards away, which hit the target; water, mud, and cement were pumped down. The well was eventually capped on November 6, 1970, 16 months after control was lost, at a cost of $2.7 million. As Gordon Jones said: "It was a tough one to start with, but it was a very spectacular start and it certainly showed people that there were a lot of hydrocarbons waiting to be found in the high Arctic."

On October 25, 1970, the first gas well on King Christian Island also blew out spectacularly: "The well caught fire," said Hetherington.

Panarctic's "blaze of glory" lights up King Christian Island. Photo provided by Panarctic Oils.

As the rig hands ran off the floor, they hit the blow-out preventer, and it momentarily shut the well in. It stopped the fire long enough that the crew could get off the rig. It held the well for about 30 seconds. We only had 150 feet of pipe in the hole, so when the gas pressure built up, it blew up beneath the pipe and put a rift in the earth 700 feet long. Then we had a curtain of fire 300 feet into the air—you could see it by airplane 300 to 400 miles away. The gas flow was estimated at 400 million cubic feet a day. It melted all the steel—the rig was gone—there was nothing left of the engines except the crankshaft. I suggested to then Minister of Indian and Northern Affairs, Jean Chretien, that he turn the incident into a positive thing, so I took presidents of oil companies to see it, to show that the Arctic definitely had energy reserves. As a result, four of the companies wanted to invest money in the area!

Eventually, the fire was doused and, again, a well close by was used to drill directionally to the wild well. Water, mud, and cement were pumped in to kill it, on January 24, 1971. The second well was completed, and became one of the largest potential gas producers in North America, with test rates up to 188 million cubic feet per day, although there was no pipeline to transport it.

At Bent Horn, the M.V. Arctic *loads crude oil destined for Montreal. Photo provided by Panarctic Oils.*

A new gas discovery was announced in December 1971—at Kristoffer Bay on Ellef Ringnes Island. It was Panarctic's fourth well and third successful wildcat. At that time, six other wells were being drilled on Panarctic lands. By the end of 1972, Panarctic Oils had drilled 26 wells in the Arctic Islands, with discoveries totalling an estimated potential volume of recoverable gas in excess of eight trillion cubic feet. The outlook for Arctic Island discoveries was bright, and millions more dollars poured into the area, on the part of both industry and government (maintaining the 55:45 percent ratio).

Oil discoveries turned out to be fewer and farther between, though no less important. The Bent Horn discovery on Cameron Island in 1974 was completed as a 500-barrel-per-day producer. Subsequent wells produced at a rate of over 5,000 barrels per day. Bent Horn supplied fuel to the Polaris mine, and its oil was also transported south, one or two tankers-full a year, to Montreal and in 1989 to European markets.

By the end of 1982, according to Bryce Cameron, 10 gas fields with estimated total proven "reserves" of 18.3 trillion cubic feet had been discovered, and estimates of oil "reserves" for three offshore reservoirs and the Bent Horn field on land amounted to 750 million barrels. One hundred and seventy wells had been drilled—an average of just one well to every 600,000 acres—with what seemed to be a clear potential for many more discoveries. But drilling declined after 1973 and stopped completely by 1988. A "modest" exploration program was proposed in 1991, but then cancelled.

Most of the land in the Panarctic deal was ultimately surrendered to the Crown. The company continued to deliver Bent Horn oil, but other work concentrated on abandonment and site restoration. Only significant discovery leases—Bent Horn, Drake Point, King Christian, and a few other locations—remained. Production at Bent Horn held out the longest—until the fall of 1996. According to Grey Alexander, who has been with Panarctic Oils for almost 30 years, the company anticipates full Arctic abandonment by year's end 1999.

Of the Panarctic venture, Gordon Jones said: "It was a rather remarkable effort, and I don't think we have ever had anything quite like it before in the Canadian oil industry, and nothing quite like it since."

Cam Sproule's vision of an Arctic Islands consortium had been realized, though he never lived to see any of its successes. Despite having little or no influence in the company by the time of his death, respect for the man and his role in the formation of Panarctic Oils was evident in the company's obituary of Cam published in their 1969 Annual Report.

Said Earl Miller:

Of some 125 wells drilled eventually in the Islands, 28 were capable of oil or gas production—a ratio of 1 in 6. Two huge gas fields were discovered on Melville and King Christian Islands and modest oil reserves were found. Today's logistics and prices still leave the Arctic out on the edge—a sleeping giant among the world's reservoirs, waiting someday to be re-awakened.

John Campbell Sproule, B.Sc., M.A., Ph.D.

Dr. J. Campbell Sproule, the founder of Panarctic passed away suddenly on May 21, 1970. The Directors and staff of Panarctic mourn the loss of this remarkable Canadian. He was one of the first to perceive the great potential of the Arctic Islands region and the opportunity available to Canadians to develop it. He pressed his convictions indefatigably, even when others faltered.

Much of the basic geological exploration was his own and it reflects his technical prowess and scientific honesty. That work, coupled with organizing ability and constant, forceful enthusiasm, showed the way to a firm beginning in the development of the region.

Panarctic Oils Ltd. owes its existence to the efforts of Dr. Sproule in bringing into association a number of companies, deliberately Canadian, and the Government of Canada to launch a major operation. It remains for us to prove with his inspiration the worth of this legacy for Canada.

Cam Sproule was internationally recognized as a scientist. He was also recognized as a warm sincere person with many interests and a concern for his fellow man. He impressed us all, and we share a great loss.

Panarctic Oils Annual Report, 1969

TRAGEDY TO TRIUMPH

NEW BEGINNINGS

As essential as knowledge and skills may be,
no amount can ever substitute for experience.

Sproule Associates Limited

The majestic Rockies rise above one of Alberta's many lakes.
Photo provided by Sproule Associates.

The End of an Era

The long-awaited shareholders' agreement presented by Cam to his Associates in the latter part of 1969 specified that when shareholders left the firm or died, the remaining shareholders would have a pre-emptive right to purchase the shares. Cam insisted on this arrangement in order to keep the company within his control, never contemplating that the clause would come into effect so soon, at his own death. "I think Sproule thought he was going to live forever," said Charlie Bulmer. "He had no intention of that applying to *him* particularly."

On May 21, 1970, Cam Sproule's life came to an abrupt end in Jasper, at an Association of Professional Engineers, Geologists and Geophysicists of Alberta (APPEGA) convention. Noel Cleland remembered that day well:

> It was the Fiftieth Annual Jubilee Meeting of APPEGA up in Jasper, and for some reason, I guess it's fortuitous, Tony and I decided that we should go to that annual meeting. We'd never been to one before, and I'd never really been involved in APPEGA business. We took our wives and drove up there. Sproule came up, and he was going to give a lecture on the geology of the Arctic—his one true love—on a Thursday afternoon, about 4:30. He was sitting in a chair showing slides of the Arctic, and it looked like he was reaching down from the chair to pick up a slide that had fallen on the floor. But he was falling off the chair, dead, in front of an audience of 30 or 40 people. They got an ambulance right away and rushed him over to the hospital and tried to get his heart going, but nothing worked ... he was dead.

Autuum comes to the Athabasca River valley in northern Alberta.
Photo provided by Lois Harding.

Cam's funeral was held on Monday, May 25 at Wesley United Church in Calgary. Flowers reportedly arrived from all over the world, filling the church, "like Easter Sunday," said daughter Judy. The active pallbearers were Stan Harding, Charlie Bulmer, Don Campbell, Tony Edgington, Noel Cleland, and Al Gorrell, Directors of Sproule at the time—the same men who would carry the company forward into a new era. Honourary pallbearers were Gus Beck, Bill Hancock, Bill Howells, Ted Link, Carl Nickle, John Noakes, Harold Riley, Gray Sharp, Wally Smith, and Jack Webb.

120

Cam's death left his employees, his friends, and his family in shock, unable to believe that someone so vital was gone. His friends were grief-stricken at the funeral, and his wife, Maude, to some extent never got over her loss.

In the years following his death, Sproule employees struggled to keep the company going, working by the principles on which Sproule was built: dedication, hard work, and honesty. Although Tony Edgington, Cam's successor as president, by all accounts did an excellent job, Cam's days as boss were never forgotten.

To add to the shock of Cam's death, Willa Tegart, his devoted secretary, died one month after him. Noel said:

> It was so close, it was unreal. She thought the sun rose and set on Sproule. She looked after him, then she just up and died weeks after him. We didn't know that she had been diagnosed with cancer.

Colin Risk, a senior petroleum engineering technician at Sproule, remembered Willa

> as the type of person that wouldn't drink, smoke or say a cuss word. She was about as straight-laced as they got. In fact, that's why it was such a surprise—this lung cancer, it came as a shock 'cause she was hardly ever sick. I was the one that was with Willa that last day. I had to take her to the hospital, and I never saw her again. It was pretty sad.

Just weeks before his death, Cam was given an Honourary Doctor of Science Degree by the University of Notre Dame at Nelson, B.C. for his contribution to geological science. He was asked to deliver the convocation address to the graduating class on May 2. Daughter Anne was surprised by what he said:

> In that speech, it was the first time I ever heard my father being personally humble about his work, and what he said was that his generation had blundered. I was astonished to sit in that audience and hear him say that it was up to the next generation to do something about the conflict between the environment and the search for oil. He saw what had happened to the Inuit way of life and what had happened to the land.

Cam was torn between his love for the land and his love of exploration. His concern for what lay ahead was evident in his words to the students. He said that it was up to their generation and those of the future

The Boss Remembered

He was the boss, there was never any doubt about that. Cam Sproule put fear in the hearts of most of his employees. If you didn't measure up, my goodness he was a tough tack—but what a man to work for, what an encouraging man. It was challenging. He didn't suffer fools gladly, and he strolled the halls with great determination. His stride was almost twice as long as the average man's, and if you were following him, it was like you were in low gear. He was a very, very tough, fit man. He impressed me as being a man who was supremely determined to get the job done, and he could not waste a moment—there wasn't time to waste a moment on trivialities.

George Hunter

I really believe he had a big talent in terms of foresight, as being a creator of things, as far as being tenacious and sticking with it. In those days, thinking back, they've got to be some of the more exciting days. There was always a cause, always a problem to be solved. I think you'll find some people who have been quite critical about him as a financial manager and a businessman. Personally, I take all that with a large grain of salt. He created a firm with an international reputation that has been very good to quite a number of engineers, geologists, and other employees over the years.

Charlie Bulmer

A.N. (Tony) Edgington
Sproule President 1970–1983

Tony studied engineering at Aberdeen University in Scotland, before serving in Her Royal Majesty's Air Force. In 1950, he graduated with a Bachelor of Science degree from the University of Missouri School of Mines and Metallurgy, and in the following years did post graduate studies at Tulsa University. He was employed by the Carter Oil Company in the United States for eight years, and joined Sproule in 1958. He became chief engineer in 1964, and shortly after, executive vice-president. Upon Cam Sproule's death in May 1970, he was appointed president.

Tony's most difficult task as president of Sproule was to enter into what became long and, at times, unpleasant negotiations with Cam's estate. The successful completion of those negotiations ensured that Sproule's remaining shareholders could acquire the company. Under his guidance, they gradually untangled the affairs of the consulting firm from the commitments left by its founder.

With his broad background in engineering, and his financial acumen, Tony showed the company the way to go, and his presidency served as a model for his successors. He stepped down from the presidency in 1983, and a year later left Sproule to pursue other interests: Earl Miller, Sproule's long-time treasurer, and Tom Cahoon, a geophysicist, are his associates in a new venture—CEM Resources Ltd.

to see to it that the outside manpower we invite to help us is carefully selected and that the development of our natural resources proceeds forthwith as usefully and effectively as it can be done.

The weight of much responsibility will be upon you, Ladies and Gentlemen of the Graduating class, as well as on others like you, for the simple reason that you are being placed in a favoured position by virtue of your education and knowledge. You must, therefore, do your part or you will not have justified your existence on Earth. ... each of you will have justified his place on Earth only if he or she does the best he can with those talents he is given.

It has been said that, "You can't take it with you," but I don't believe that. I believe firmly that you will take with you for all of the Time—that which you have left behind. May you all be able to take pride in what you leave behind!

According to Judy, after Cam's death her mother was approached by the University of Calgary with a request to name the new Earth Sciences building after Cam. "Regretfully, mother was grief-stricken and told them she did not want any monuments."

The monument to Cam, however, was the company he had built for 19 years. By 1970, Sproule had become the largest geological and petroleum engineering consulting company in the country; highly regarded not only in Canada but throughout the world.

Transition and Change

Eighteen days after Cam's death, Tony Edgington was appointed president. Stan Harding became senior vice-president, and Don Campbell became vice-president. Noel Cleland was appointed chief engineer three months later. (Stan retired within two years of Cam's death, and Noel was made vice-president in his place.)

Tony's first task as president was to negotiate with Cam's estate for ownership of the company. The process proved to be a long and arduous one. The executors of Cam's estate were Montreal Trust, and it became apparent during discussions that they did not recognize that, as a consulting practice, Sproule was a company made up of, as Tony, himself, said, "active participants doing the work, and not a bunch of salaried investors sitting in the background." Therefore, the point was made that if the executors did not wish to negotiate, Tony and the other shareholders could simply walk away and start a new company.

But they had no desire to do so. The Sproule name carried a lot of weight in the industry, and they had contributed to that reputation. "We had a high regard for Cam as an individual," said Tony, "and as a geologist and a visionary."

> He had created this practice. He built it to a certain point. Some of us had participated with him in building it. We devoted a lot of time and effort in bringing it to where it was. You don't want to see what you've worked for dissipated and have to start again and try to create a new entity. We knew what his dreams and ambitions were, and we wanted to take what we had at that time and build on that foundation, and go on to do the best possible thing we could with this well-regarded name.

"Walking" was only an alternative if, and only if, Montreal Trust demanded an unreasonably high price for Cam's shares. Under the terms of the shareholders' agreement, the price for the shares was to be set by Price Waterhouse based on that firm's evaluation of the fair value of the company. The Price Waterhouse evaluation caused significant conflict among Montreal Trust, Cam's family, and the shareholders. The value attributed to the shares was much lower than the estate's executors and the family anticipated. The evaluation had taken into account the direct and contingent liabilities incurred by the consulting firm with respect to Northward Aviation. In addition, the Arctic exploratory work had cost the firm huge amounts of money: Sproule field parties had operated at a loss for several years. Thus, the price per share was modest, particularly in the minds of Montreal Trust. Legal counsel expressed the possibility of litigation over the Price Waterhouse evaluation, despite the clear provisions of the company's Articles of Association. Some surmised that Cam, characteristically optimistic, had painted a rosier financial picture of the company than was actually the case.

The Sproule shareholders sought their own legal advice, which confirmed their position, but serious consideration was given again to the possibility of walking away and starting their own firm, rather than entering into a costly legal battle. Fortunately, saner heads on both sides prevailed. Despite some antagonism and frustration along the way, a deal was finally reached, and the shareholders bought Cam's shares and agreed to take on the liability of Northward. "Everything was very amicable among the shareholders," said Tony. "We had no dissension at all between the geological and the engineering side. There was complete harmony, and I think an identity of interest in where we wanted to go."

Charlie Bulmer recalled the day of reckoning, when each shareholder had to come up with the money to purchase the shares:

> For me personally, a fairly young fellow, it seemed like an awful lot of money that I had to sign for at the bank. I don't think anybody today recognizes the risk we were taking in going into debt and buying the firm. It is a different situation today, when the company shows a history of profits and stability.

Once the shares were purchased, it was agreed that Maude would remain chairman of the Board. It was an honourary position, with no shareholding or direct participation in the company, and it lasted for one year.

Tony, with Earl Miller's assistance, spent the first four years of his presidency putting the affairs of the consultancy in order. One of the most time-consuming aspects of this was the running of Northward Aviation. Earl and Tony re-arranged its financial affairs, and it became an independent operation in its own right, with Earl as president.

The End of Field Exploration

Stan Harding retired in 1973, and Don Campbell was appointed manager of the geological exploration department; Noel Cleland was made manager of engineering, and Charlie Bulmer became manager of the geological evaluations department. The following year, the company changed its name to Sproule Associates Limited and moved its offices to the Alberta Wheat Pool building, to avoid the high rent for the Bow Building imposed by its manager, Montreal Trust.

That same year marked the end of an era for the company: Sproule's surface geology department, at one time its biggest department, was losing money at an unprecedented rate; the expertise and services of Don's department were no longer in high demand. The days of large-scale surface exploration field parties were winding down in the Arctic Islands; everyone was moving into the seismic and drilling phase. Don and Tony found themselves looking at other areas of the world, where opportunities to conduct large-scale field programs might exist. In 1974, an opportunity

Sproule at Play

Sproule employees know well that they are expected to work hard; many put in long hours and give up portions of their weekends to complete reports on time. But the company is not all work and no play: a dedicated social committee ensures that the Sproule "gang" takes a break from routine to get to know each other in a non-working setting.

Golf, softball, and hockey bring out the more athletic of the group, and Sproule wouldn't be a Calgary company without a barbeque at Stampede time. Special family events are also planned for the children. Of course, the company treats its employees to an extravagant Christmas party. Back in Cam's day, unable to find adequate facilities after an 11th-hour decision to have a party, arrangements were made to hold it after Christmas. The company continues the tradition today; the party is usually held in February, after work pressures have subsided and the Christmas rush is over.

Photos provided by Sproule Associates.

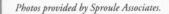

Coalbed Methane

When the energy crisis hit in the mid 1970s, oil and gas companies started looking for an alternative non-conventional resource. Coalbed methane (CBM) came into vogue within certain companies in the United States. Calgary-based companies with coal departments followed with their own CBM research. One company, Nova Corporation of Alberta, set up a subsidiary called Algas Resources Limited, who in turn engaged Sproule to help manage its field drilling program and determine the potential extraction of methane gas. Over the next five years, $12 million was spent drilling 12 research wells and two production wells in the southern foothills of Alberta. An important outcome of this research was the development of the cavitation method, a new type of well completion currently being successfully used around the world.

Recently, Sproule managed the technical side of Fracmaster's coalbed methane projects overseas; in Hungary (1993) and Czech Republic (1993-94). Technical assessments were also completed in Poland, Ukraine, Spain, and Russia in the early 1990s. The work lasted four years, with Rudy Cech, current vice-president of geology, leading the project. Despite millions of dollars spent by Fracmaster, the work did not lead to production, probably because of unexpected low flowrates and a reluctance to spend more money, according to Rudy. The Fracmaster work did, however, lead to a number of projects in eastern Europe with other local companies wanting to move into the foreign market.

Today, Sproule manages the Canadian Coalbed Methane Forum, which is a consortium of 28 Calgary-based companies that share current CBM data. Sproule offers its expertise in coalbed methane through a course entitled "An Introduction to Coalbed Methane Extraction," taught by Rudy Cech and Keith MacLeod.

arose to conduct surface geological studies over a large area of southeastern Iran—a ten million dollar project—and Sproule spent considerable time, and money, preparing a proposal. Their bid was unsuccessful, and, in retrospect, political turmoil, together with fluctuation in oil prices, would probably have meant substantial losses to Sproule.

It became apparent, according to Charlie, that foreign work was a high-risk business:

> It was a big game we were playing, and we weren't sure about the political and economic climate in the areas in which we were operating. We didn't know, for example, if we ever would get paid. If we were going to run the same type of field operation that we were used to running in the Arctic Islands, we could spend an awful lot of money setting up field programs and then not get paid, and it could sink the whole ship.

As a result, it was decided that the promotion of large-scale field operations would end. If Sproule was going to do any international work, it would be done on a smaller scale, using one or two people only, so that the whole firm would not be at risk.

In subsequent years, many foreign projects were completed, the majority for international agencies such as the World Bank, the UN Development Bank, and the Commonwealth Secretariat; others were for private clients. These involved both engineers and geologists (often Tony Edgington, Al Gorrell, and Stan Harding), usually to assess the resource potential and economics of the various areas.

Shutting down the surface department was not an easy decision for Tony and the other directors to make. Don Campbell had played a big role in promoting international work. He left Sproule and started his own consulting firm, and many of Sproule's other geologists followed, leaving the surface geology department a skeleton of its former self. Charlie became vice-president of geology in June 1974.

Cam no doubt would have agonized over the loss of the department closest to his heart, and may have tried to take on the foreign work. However, Tony was cut from different cloth, and he saw a future in engineering evaluations. The days of big exploration programs, like those undertaken in the Arctic Islands, were at an end.

Back to Business

With the business of Cam's estate successfully concluded, and the surface department prospects diminished, the company changed its focus to large-scale oil and gas evaluations. Some of the projects Sproule undertook in the 1970s were significant, not only in terms of the work involved and the income generated, but also in terms of establishing the reputation of the company and showing the industry Sproule was moving ahead, despite the loss of its founder.

A project for Pan Alberta was one of the biggest geological and engineering jobs Sproule has ever undertaken. Morris Kilik, a petroleum engineer, and Bob Blair, president of Alberta Gas Trunk Line Co. (AGTL, now known as Nova), formed Pan Alberta Gas with the idea of supplying the gas market for five years with a "southern pre-build" of the northern pipeline from the Mackenzie Delta. At the time, it was estimated that it would take five years to construct the northern part. Kilik and Blair approached Tony Edgington, Noel Cleland, and Charlie Bulmer with a proposal that Sproule do the reserves and deliverability analyses for the export of the gas. An enormous amount of data from approximately 400 companies came in to Pan Alberta, and was passed on to Sproule for evaluation.

At the end of 1973, Pan Alberta filed an application to the Energy Resources and Conservation Board (ERCB) for a permit to remove the gas from Alberta. "Most of the volume of the application consisted of Sproule reserves and deliverability estimates, location maps, and geological maps, where necessary," Kilik said. "Due to the size of each copy of the application, which had orange covers, the application was dubbed the 'Big Yellow Bible.'"

The ERCB gave its decision in February 1974, recommending approval by the Minister of Energy and the government. The reserves estimated by Sproule were within two percent of what the ERCB estimated in its conclusions. An Order-in-Council was signed by Premier Lougheed in July 1974, authorizing the removal of gas from fields in the province of Alberta. Sales contracts were ultimately signed with Northwest Pipeline Corp. of Salt Lake City, Utah; Pacific Lighting Gas Development Company of Los Angeles, California; and United Gas Pipeline Company of Houston, Texas. Sproule's reserve estimates were again placed under scrutiny by these companies, to satisfy themselves that ample reserves existed to fulfil contract requirements.

First Oil

Like the Canadian Pacific Railway, the Canadian National Railway was given freehold land by the Crown, essentially for "opening up" the west. The CPR got into the oil and gas industry at an early stage, forming Canadian Pacific Oil and Gas (CPOG), which later became PanCanadian. The CNR, however, did not follow in their footsteps, opting instead to lease its lands to oil and gas companies out of its real estate office in Winnipeg. The CNR received a cash bonus for the leases and retained a freehold royalty on any oil and gas production from the lands. J.C. Sproule and Associates had a long-standing retainer with them to advise on leasing offers and to establish bonus levels, royalty rates, and drilling commitments. Early on, Cam had encouraged them to form an oil company, and later, Charlie Bulmer, then head of the geological subsurface department (who handled the requests for CNR leases), travelled to Montreal to address members of their Board of Directors on the benefits of forming an oil and gas company to develop the CNR's own properties. However, they were not yet ready to cope with exploration risks.

Meanwhile, the Saskatchewan government introduced a more onerous mineral tax on freehold oil and gas rights. The CNR placed a moratorium on leasing its lands while it planned how to deal with changing economics associated with them. During this moratorium, a Bakken sandstone oil pool was being developed, offsetting a half-section of one of their freehold lands in the Cactus Lake area of west-central Saskatchewan. By this time, the responsibility for the CNR's mineral titles had been moved out of Winnipeg's real estate office, and John Prairie handled enquiries out of Montreal. Crown sales in Saskatchewan at that time allowed a combination of bonus and "net royalty bids." A company could offer the government a high royalty for a sales parcel with good potential. The government would then have to choose either a bonus paid at that time or potential future royalty revenues.

When the development surrounded the CNR half-section, it became apparent to a number of companies operating in the area that it could be a valuable acquisition, with little risk. Several made offers to the CNR containing "net royalty" provisions of 35 to 40 percent. Sproule's evaluation indicated that a company could afford a royalty of 70 percent and still make a reasonable return on its investment. Believing that it was an ideal opportunity for the CNR to finally become an active participant in the oil industry, Charlie suggested to John Prairie (who travelled to Calgary to review results of the Sproule analysis) that if companies could make a profit at that royalty rate, the CNR would benefit the most by drilling the property itself. John was concerned that they had no staff or experience to deal with the project, but it was explained that any services required to drill the wells, including Sproule consulting services, could be hired.

"John Prairie was quite a guy," said Glenn Robinson. "He knew nothing about the oil business, but he worked extremely hard to try and figure out how this all worked." Sproule hired Jerry Werenka as a consultant to handle the operations and do the drilling work. Frank O'Shea took care of the engineering, and geologist Wayne Moore was later hired to handle Cactus Lake, as well as to assess other CNR lands.

When the first well was drilled, Sproule was determined to do everything right. "We used the best tools, the best of everything," said Glenn. They cored the formation, just to be sure everything was as it should be. "Everyone thought we were crazy. The Bakken sand is very friable; the formation tends to crumble, and you are apt to get the core barrel stuck in the well." But it worked, and when they pulled the core, Prairie wiped a handful of oil from it.

It was the CNR's first oil, and employees celebrated that night with champagne and crackers. The next day they ran a drillstem test, to get an oil sample from the reservoir. This was a risky business because of the nature of the formation. Knowing something about the pressure in the formation, Glenn predicted how high the reservoir fluid would rise in the drillpipe:

When we pulled the drillstem test, I was showing John how smart I was—that I could estimate which section of drillpipe would contain the oil. I was right on! But when we "popped the tool" water gushed out. I said to him, "Don't worry about that. That water is just mud filtrate." We

John Prairie flashes a hand covered in oil from the core. Chris Pollok stands to his left, and Jerry Werenka is in the foreground. Photo provided by J. Glenn Robinson.

took a few more singles out only to recover more water. It kept getting cleaner…and cleaner…and we pulled a full string of water!

Glenn hurried to the engineering shack to look again at the logs. Jerry assured him he had tallied properly out of the hole. The mood was pretty discouraging out at the rig. That's when wellsite geologist Chris Pollok, said, "This is a fantastic well. It's a scientific success. It's just too bad it produces nothing but salt water!" John Prairie was not impressed.

After a few long minutes, Jerry sheepishly returned to Glenn with the answer. When they had pulled the core barrel out of the hole the night before, they had laid down a single (30 feet of drillpipe) and hadn't put it back in the string. Since he didn't tally on the way in the next day, they had tested a zone 30 feet too high. Glenn immediately looked at the log and right above the production zone was a little sand that was "soakin' wet." Glenn said to Jerry, "You clean the hole up—we're running pipe!" They called him "salt-water Robinson" for a few days, but the well is still producing.

The CNR (more correctly, CN Exploration) was now in the oil and gas business. Sproule went on to supervise the drilling of seven more wells on that half section of land, continued to manage the field, and helped CN look at other developments. Some time later, CN hired its own manager, (they had up to 30 wells by this time) and opened up a Calgary office; Frank O'Shea and Wayne Moore left Sproule to join them.

The Pan Alberta project and the work that spun off it helped Sproule get through the tumultuous times following Cam's death. The size of the project, and the excellent response to Sproule's work, set the company on course for the decade to come.

As the oil and gas industry changed through the 1970s and 1980s, so did the areas in which Sproule undertook work. The first major amalgamation of companies they were involved in was that of Canadian Superior Oil and Alminex in 1977, a high profile merger in Calgary. They got into the divestiture business in 1988, when Canterra Energy wanted sales packages prepared for hundreds of millions of dollars worth of assets. Sproule's involvement with clients also included managing oil and gas interests, creating "plays," and recommending prospects. They directed exploration and development operations and acted as technical advisors in a variety of situations, including reviewing proposals.

Expert Witness Work

In 1973, Sproule was retained by Charlie Baer, the trustee in bankruptcy for King Resources, to provide an evaluation of the oil and gas interests of that company in the Canadian Arctic Islands. King Resources was a Denver-based exploration company with operations in Canada, and the company had run into financial difficulties as a result of its drilling efforts in the Arctic. Under the United States Federal Bankruptcy Act, the District Court of Colorado, sitting in Denver, was required to determine for King's creditors whether or not King was actually bankrupt. In order to determine its financial situation, an evaluation of its Arctic properties had to be submitted to the Court.

When Sproule completed the evaluation, Charlie Bulmer and engineer Mike Brusset appeared as witnesses before the Honourable Fred M. Winner in Denver, to present and defend the evaluation of King Resources' Arctic holdings. Accompanying them was Jim Chilton, who had also worked on the project. Their first appearance in court was on December 5, 1973, and the second on March 14, 1974, for further cross-examination on the same matter.

In August 1977, in a continuation of the same hearing, Jim Powell, Jim Terrill, Jim Chilton, Noel Cleland, and Charlie went to Denver to present and defend revised evaluations prepared on behalf of the trustee. In discussions before the hearing, the trustee's lawyer chose Noel to present Sproule's evidence, probably, said Charlie, "because of Noel's positive manner in presenting himself, and his knowledge and definite opinions." Noel was not familiar with the geological aspects of the work, and the geological contingent "burned the midnight oil" with him to prepare him.

Judge Fred Winner wrote:

The Sproule report dealing with values in the Canadian Arctic utilizes an unconventional approach to value. I share with Mr. Sterling an inability to understand it the first time I heard it.

I have gone back and read it and reread it since, and it is one of the most interesting value approaches I have ever seen in my life, and in the course of my lifetime I have spent some time on value matters. I think it's a valid one, although I have never seen it used before.

But there is absolutely no accepted valuation approach which can be used on these properties. No appraisal method which is to be found in any text book will fit these problems. One of the witnesses said -- and I say this somewhat lightheartedly, but it is a very excellent expression of the problem -- one of the witnesses said he didn't know how to appraise an iceberg, and that's just what the problem is. You're appraising onshore and offshore in the Canadian Arctic ...

In the area to be valued ... 8 out of 103 wild cat wells were successful. That's not a very good prospect. The wells were extraordinarily expensive. There has never been a discovery of one cubic foot of gas or one barrel of oil on any land in which King has an interest.

With that, then, Sproule used this thoughtful, and I think novel, approach to value. They were confronted with the problem of trying to put a value on wild cat wells to be drilled somewhere in the Arctic sometime in the future, and that is not the easiest thing in the world to do...

... that you can appraise the values in the Canadian Arctic is to say that you can attend the County Fair with your crystal ball, because that is absolutely the only possible way you can come up with a result ...

The Sproule report, as I mentioned, attempts to update its earlier valuation of the Canadian Arctic, and as I have mentioned, it concludes that there has been a reduction in value.

N.A. (Noel) Cleland
Sproule President 1983–1992

Noel Cleland arrived in Canada from Sydney, Australia in 1954 after graduating from the University of Sydney with a degree in mining and metallurgy. He landed his first job in Canada as a drilling engineer for California Standard (later Chevron) in Calgary. After a stint in Manitoba, Noel joined Hudson's Bay Oil and Gas back in Calgary, first as a production engineer, then later as a reservoir engineer. In 1966, he accepted a position at Sproule, saying later the decision to join Sproule was one of the luckiest things he ever did. He became a Director of Sproule two years after his arrival. In 1983, when Tony Edgington stepped down, Noel became president.

Although modest when discussing his accomplishments, Noel was proud of the fact that during the period 1990-1991, when Sproule began to suffer the effects of an economic downturn, they were able, through salary cuts to both senior and junior shareholders, to avoid laying off any employees; there was no change in salary to non-shareholders.

Noel proved to be an expert in economic programs and in using discounted cash flows to evaluate oil and gas investment opportunities. He significantly expanded the engineering department and excelled at getting Sproule's name out to the industry. He also served as president of both the CIM and APEGGA during his tenure at Sproule. Noel officially retired from Sproule in September 1994, but continues to consult for the company from time to time.

The methodology used to formulate the report is one based upon theory of probability. It was one that I -- as I have already mentioned, I have extreme difficulty following. I now understand it -- I think. I believe it's valid. I think it's accurate. I think it's a novel, imaginative way to approach the probability of finding gas or oil somewhere on the 23,687,733 acres of land and water in which King has an interest. I think it meets all the tests of <u>Consolidated Rock Products,</u> and I think the United States Supreme Court will, if it ever gets a chance, accept it if the United States Supreme Court is confronted with the facts we are confronted with here.

In the end, the Judge assigned a value to the properties consistent with the Sproule evaluation.

Down Under in the Potash Mines of Saskatchewan

The company was involved in potash work even in Cam Sproule's day, with both Stan Harding and Al Gorrell doing evaluations of potash reserves. Wayne Sargent, current geologist and shareholder, with Sproule since 1982, has been doing work with potash mines since 1987.

A project for International Minerals and Chemical Corporation started out as a preliminary assessment of the reservoir within the Dawson Bay Formation. The potential of salt water invasion into their facility at Esterhazy, Saskatchewan, had to be determined—fractures large enough to climb into had developed, some well over a 100 feet above the level of the mine, and some 1,200 or 1,400 feet in length.

The project started off as a simple job, until the client requested that structural geology be done, to map various features seen underground and to try to determine what had caused the inflow of brine into the mine. In the course of the next six years, Wayne spent up to a third of his time working on that project. "There was a lot of time spent in Saskatchewan," he said. "I had three birthdays in a row at the Hazy-Hilton. The waitresses would ply me with cupcakes stuffed with candles."

Wayne enjoys the cramped quarters of a fracture above the Esterhazy mine workings. Photo provided by Wayne Sargent.

One day I was bringing a rather large gentleman into one of the areas, to show him where the water was coming in. We climbed up from the mine workings and through a very narrow channel. I knew that in places it was very, very tight, so I told him to go in ahead of me. He was large, and if he got stuck, I wanted to make sure I could back out—I didn't want to suffocate while he was wedged in the hole behind me. The end of the tunnel was about 300 feet in from where we had started. We had to crawl on our belly—very, very slowly, because things are scraping on both sides and you can't lift your head to see where you're going.

He was ahead of me and talking to me, and all of a sudden I couldn't hear him any longer and I could see with my headlamp his feet flopping in front of my face. There was absolute silence, and he wiggled and struggled and finally got on a little further, and we came to the hole at the end. It was an area about a foot and a half high, just about as high as a coffee table, and about eight feet across. He was curled up in there like a puppy in a basket. He said to me, "Is that the only way out —the way we came in?" And I said, "Yeah, it is." He was afraid to go out. I said, "Well, I'll tell you what, just so that it will be safe, I'll go out first and you can follow me." I didn't want to get stuck myself!

It was a two-mine complex at Esterhazy—K1 and K2—joined together by a five-mile underground roadway. There were about 1,500 miles of roadway in that particular mine: "You needed a map, or you'd get lost, because your sense of direction was the pits underground," said Wayne. "There are no stars that you can see, and everything is black unless you've got your headlamp or the lights on the vehicle."

On one occasion, we climbed into an area about 100 feet above the mine workings, and they hadn't actually stabilized this particular cavern. There were no timbers to climb up on or anything. You had to wiggle between the walls of the cavern. We got up to just about where we wanted to be when my headlamp died. The mine geologist who was with me had to take my lamp and return to a staging point outside of this particular area to exchange lamps with someone else. I was left alone for close to half an hour in total darkness. You can't see anything, you can hear water dripping, and that's about the only thing you can hear other than pieces of rock falling off around you from time to time. And I was sweating—it was quite hot and very, very stuffy. ... It's for people who can live with themselves—I'll put it that way.

Sproule's work in Esterhazy ended when International settled with its insurance company, just before they went to court over a lawsuit concerning lost production due to brine inflow.

> ### *Potash White Noise*
>
> *When you walk into a freshly mined area and you stand very, very quietly, it sounds like you are in a giant bowl of Rice Krispies. Because of the pressure release on the rocks, little particles— almost needle-like—flake off or fall off the rock face and you can hear them tinkling down onto the mine workings. But it's coming all around you—it's the most incredible noise as the pressure is being released into the mine workings from the host rock.*
>
> *Wayne Sargent*

(top) Bruce Marshall engages his students' attention at the Sproule offices.
(bottom) Students watch operations at the drilling rig first hand. Photos provided by Roger Thomsen.

Teaching What They Know

As early as 1961, Cam recognized that the investment community knew very little about the oil business, despite its being a primary stakeholder in it. He knew the value, to both his company and to the industry as a whole, of an educational program that introduced Sproule's techniques of evaluating oil and gas properties. In 1963, the Alberta Society of Petroleum Geologists asked the University of Calgary (U of C) to develop a course on economics for geologists. The university, in turn, asked Sproule to prepare and present it, and the first course was presented in the fall of 1963.

The U of C Department of Continuing Education course was originally developed by Clarence Winter (a Sproule engineer), Tony Edgington, and Charlie Bulmer. Initially, only geologists registered for the course, which was entitled "Economics for Geologists." After a time, Sproule saw the opportunity to expand its education services, and offered an accompanying course for engineers.

When Glenn Robinson joined Sproule in 1973, Noel Cleland and Mike Brusset were teaching a course at the U of C, then entitled "Economic Evaluations in Petroleum Engineering." Glenn took over from Mike some time later, and Bruce Marshall, John Carlson, Nora Stewart, and Keith MacLeod, on the engineering side, have been teaching this and other courses for a number of years. On the geological side, Douglas Carsted, John Chipperfield, and Wayne Sargent have "filled the bill." The 12-week course, now entitled "Evaluation of Canadian Oil and Gas Properties," continues to be taught twice a year.

Sproule expanded its education services considerably beyond the U of C course, offering spring and fall seminars in Calgary, primarily targeted to the financial community. Seminars are a week long, and people from all over Canada, the United States, and overseas, including Russia and Hong Kong, have attended the course.

In addition to the U of C course and the in-house seminar, Sproule has taught the evaluation course to various companies, at their request. The Canadian Institute of Mining and Metallurgy retained Sproule to teach both a five-day basic course, for geologists and engineers just getting into the evaluation business, and a three-day advanced course, for management-level professionals. The Canadian Society of

Petroleum Geologists (CSPG) also approached Sproule about a course on risk analysis. "Texaco wanted a course for its geologists that would assist them on assigning probablities to their exploration plays," said Glenn. "Our answer was 'How can we do that?' Nobody knows the probability of finding oil and gas on a prospect. Mother Nature never told us the rules. She made the world, then threw away the manual!" To meet the demand, Glenn wrote the basis for a course, entitled "Risk Analysis of Canadian Oil and Gas Properties," over a six-week sabbatical leave.

The International Marketplace

The company's first foreign assignment came in 1963, during Cam Sproule's time, when Stan Harding took on work for the United Nations (U.N.). Brazil was seeking financial aid to construct a caustic soda plant and wanted to know if the scheme was practical. Stan remembered leaving New York and someone advising him, "If you have anything negative to say, don't say it until you get out of the country."

After spending a month in Brazil, Stan recommended a plant be constructed, not in the state that had originally submitted the proposal, but in a neighbouring one. Stan was told later that it almost started a civil war. But the country soon forgot about the caustic soda plant after reading Stan's report, because he had mentioned evidence of potash in the area. In 1964, Cam, himself, was back in Brazil discussing potash. A caustic soda plant *was* built in Brazil in the early 1970s by Union Carbide—an $8 million plant, Stan recalled, and at the location he had recommended.

In the late 1960s, Stan also travelled to Poland on behalf of the United Nations Technical Assistance program. He was to review Poland's natural resource industries to see if there was any area for which they could receive assistance from the U.N.; eventually, they asked for and received aid for potash exploration. Sproule also worked in Morocco, Guatemala, Indonesia, Belize, and Australia, and Cam, himself, went to India.

When the work for Pan Alberta began in 1972, Sproule's attention focused on the domestic market, although international work continued. Sproule undertook projects in the 1970s in Australia, India, Pakistan, the Middle East, Africa, Europe, and South America. An unusual job in the mid-1970s involved the search for coarse sand in Kuwait: the desert sand was too fine for concrete. It was such a problem, remembered Rudy Cech, that a "discovery" would "disappear" overnight!

Al Gorrell undertook a number of international projects for the United Nations and the World Bank. He travelled extensively during the years he was with Sproule, becoming an expert in areas as

Harold Alvin Gorrell, 1924–1985

H.A. (Al) Gorrell died in a fire which swept through the Regent Hotel in Manila, Philippines, on February 12, 1985. On a consulting assignment with the Asian Development Bank for Sproule Associates Limited, he had stopped off in Manila to visit bank officers on his return from a visit to a gas field in Pakistan.

Al Gorrell was born January 30, 1924, in Crystal City, Manitoba, where he attended primary school and his first two years of high school. After completing senior matriculation at the high school in Geraldton, Ontario, Al enlisted in the Royal Canadian Air Force in 1942 and served as an aircrew Flying Officer with Bomber Command in England. At the end of World War II, he returned to Ontario and entered the University of Toronto where he received a B.A. (honours geology) in 1950 and an M.A. (stratigraphy) in 1952.

During 1951 and 1952, Al worked as a petroleum geologist for Imperial Oil Limited in Chatham, Ontario, then headed west to Regina in August 1952 to join Tidewater Oil Company as a senior stratigrapher. During that time he began his early research into subsurface waters and their chemistry and studies of evaporite deposits. These studies were his continuing specialty, for which he attained a well-deserved reputation as a most knowledgeable expert.

In January 1957, Al came to Calgary where he joined Sproule. During his long career with the company, he worked in all phases of petroleum geology and also continued his research and studies in evaporite and industrial minerals and subsurface waters, including studies of geothermal potential. His work took him to all areas of North America,

Africa, Australia, South America, the Middle East, and the Orient. He had been a senior staff member of Sproule for many years and served as a director and corporate secretary since 1970.

Al was a member of the following technical societies and associations: American Association of Petroleum Geologists (Certified Petroleum Geologist), Association of Professional Engineers, Geologists and Geophysicists of Alberta (Professional Geologist), Canadian Geothermal Resources Association, Canadian Institute of Mining and Metallurgy, Canadian Society of Petroleum Geologists, Canadian Well Logging Society, Geological Association of Canada (Fellow), Geological Society of America (Fellow), Society of Economic Geologists, and Society of Economic Paleontologists and Mineralogists.

Al was the author of many technical papers in various journals during the past 20 years. Most of the publications dealt with subsurface waters and their association with oil and gas accumulations, evaporite deposits, waste disposal, and geothermal applications.

Al is survived by his wife, Jean, and his mother, Margaret, both of Calgary.

C.A.S. Bulmer, March 1985

diverse as subsurface waters and evaporite and geothermal deposits. On a return trip from one of his overseas assignments to Pakistan for the Asian Development Bank, Gorrell stopped off in Manila, Philippines to visit some bank officers. On February 12, 1985, Al died as a result of a terrorist's fire in the Regent Hotel where he was staying. The *Calgary Herald* (February 14, 1985) reported that a group calling itself "The Angels" claimed responsibility for the blaze, in protest against United States-Japan support for Philippine president Ferdinand Marcos.

In the late 1980s, Sproule experienced a slow period on the domestic front, so a push was made for even more international work. In the 1990s, the company gained a substantial foothold in China and Russia. "The world market today is that it isn't that easy now to just go and find oil and gas anywhere in the world," said Glenn. "Companies and governments are now becoming aware that you have to apply good economic analysis to oil and gas opportunities before you can proceed."

> Interestingly, many oil- and gas-producing countries lack the economic knowledge they need because they have little experience with difficult conditions. In the Middle East, there aren't many wells, even though they produce about 60 to 70 percent of the world's oil. They don't really know anything about risk analysis. They stick a hole down there and whoosh, up it comes! They don't have to know a lot about technology, because it's easy. In Canada it's tough, because we have very low producers, and our geology is tough, and our climatic conditions are tough, and everything we do over here is hard. Our economics are tough. So we have to be good.

Under Sproule's current president, foreign business has been actively pursued. International work, however, is not always a bed of roses. Cultural differences in the way business is done outside of Canada can be a challenge. For a company like Sproule, who must maintain an objective point of view, it is especially difficult because it "involves a lot of personal contact and making deals," said Rudy Cech.

> We find it very restrictive, because we need to keep at arm's length and maintain our independence. International work is done on specs, on promotions, on promises of future deals: "You do this work and I'll give you interests in the project afterward." We can't take interests because we will lose our independence. And we can't make "deals" and then be objective with banks and securities commissions.

Opportunities overseas have often been the result of timing: political change in the communist block in the early 1990s opened up considerable opportunity in Eastern Europe. "It was a lucky time for us," admits Rudy. "The projects we have had would probably not have happened without those changes." And socio-economic change opened up even more:

Working Overseas

WHAT IT IS <u>NOT</u>

(A) A Paid holiday.

(B) An assignment for junior staff or someone who you cannot use effectively in your home office.

(C) Something you get by writing a letter to the United Nations expressing a general interest in foreign consulting.

(D) A big money-maker.

(E) A soft touch.

WHAT IT IS

(A) Usually an assignment for a fully competent and recognized specialist.

(B) Generally an assignment of less than four months of one or two people.

(C) Hard work involving special technical problems and unfamiliar local situations.

(D) Work for which you must compete effectively against many of the world's most technically competent people with experience abroad, and against subsidized agencies who can and do provide assistance free or at very low rates.

Al Gorrell

Many countries started privatizing the oil industry: first Argentina, then Venezuela, Colombia, and Bolivia. They are now opening up to foreign investors. After the Gulf War, more Middle East countries are opening up and refinancing their promised projects.

According to Rudy, most of Sproule's international projects involve evaluation of existing fields in order to determine the potential for increasing their production.

> In the late 1980s, most of these countries were experiencing low prices. They neglected for a long time to go back to their own fields and put money in them. Russia is probably the most extreme example of long-term neglect of their oil industry. Their fields were producing, but nothing was being put back. Here in North America, a company would invest back in their fields and maintain them.

With no funds available domestically, companies and governments look to foreign investors to put money into their oil and gas industry. Sproule usually works for those investors, rather than directly for the companies or governments. In some cases, they are evaluating reserves using information dating to the 1950s. "We are spoiled here in Canada," said Rudy, "especially here in Alberta. We have a huge amount of data available publicly, to anyone. In other countries we are often looking at 'antique stuff.'"

Despite the fact that most international work deals with existing fields, Wayne Sargent, Sproule's expert in evaluating oil and gas interests in exploratory properties, is very busy:

> The past two years, our international projects have become very, very important. In 1997, close to 90 percent of my time has been with international projects, looking at undeveloped lands. Clients want to know what the property might be worth under certain scenarios, how much it's going to cost to develop it, where they can sell any hydrocarbons that they might encounter, and what it could be worth to them in today's marketplace.

There is no question in Rudy's mind that getting into the international marketplace has been worthwhile. In 1994, Sproule Associates Limited recognized the growth of the international side of the company and formed a wholly owned subsidiary—Sproule International Limited. Then, in 1997, an office was opened in Denver, Colorado, and another wholly owned subsidiary—Sproule Associates Inc.—was formed to better deal with a growing American market.

The Great "Door" of China

According to Glenn Robinson, one of the biggest jobs the company has ever undertaken was in

---

Adventures Abroad

We are flying from Russia to Donetsk, a coal-mining town in Ukraine, to do a preliminary analysis of the gas potential. We had one day in Moscow; it was a Sunday, October 3, 1993, so we take a tour in the morning, and drive to all the usual places, like Red Square, taking pictures of all the sites. In the afternoon, we are to leave Moscow for Ukraine. We are driving to the airport, and the streets are empty. And we wonder why nothing was happening. We get to the airport, and nobody's there. After an hour of waiting, a guy comes and takes us out the back doors to the plane that was flying to Ukraine. When we land there, we find out that armed rebels had taken the "White House" in Moscow. The next day, October 4, the army shelled it— 100 people were killed in the process. The streets had been empty because tanks were blocking the access of the army. We hadn't seen anything. We were actually right in front of the House taking pictures. If something had happened at that time, we would have been right in the middle of it.

Rudy Cech

China. In March 1992, Sproule received a request from the Sichuan Petroleum Administration (SPA) to do a gas assessment study in Sichuan province, in south-central China. The SPA was required to submit a report to the World Bank, who would consider lending them the money needed for the development. The World Bank required a third-party assessment to establish the presence of natural gas, to assess its producibility, and to estimate the cost of development. There were 15 gas fields that needed further development. A number of the fields had been drilled—deep wells with very complex geological settings and difficult reservoirs. SPA needed to build pipelines to market the gas, and to further develop the gas pools. In addition to the normal evaluation that Sproule does, SPA also wanted detailed reservoir simulation to determine how the reservoir would perform, and in several fields they were considering fracturing and stimulating low-producing wells. Finally, they wanted some new wells examined to be sure they were producing at their highest capacity.

Glenn felt Sproule's chance of being awarded the work was poor. "We were lacking expertise in reservoir simulation and in wellbore stimulation. I felt there were probably other companies in the world who had the expertise in all the areas." Then the idea of teaming up with appropriate experts in Calgary was explored. Bob Porteous of Porteous Engineering, and Roberto Aguilera of Servipetrol, were invited to join Sproule in the proposal, to provide wellbore stimulation and reservoir simulation, respectively. A very detailed proposal was written, according to World Bank specifications, for the SPA, which is the administrative arm of the Chinese National Petroleum Corporation (the oil company of China). Sproule was awarded the project, and once the report was completed, it was presented to the client's top people, who

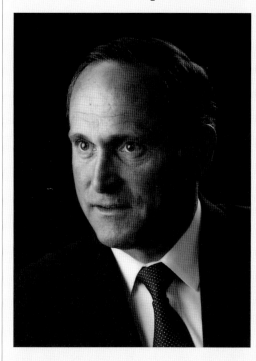

J.G. (Glenn) Robinson
Sproule President 1992–Present

J. Glenn Robinson grew up on a farm in the Ottawa valley, and became a pre-science student in engineering at the University of Ottawa. He transferred to Queen's University in Kingston and continued his engineering program there. Glenn's first job as an engineer was with the exploitation group at Shell, and a little over five years later, he got into the simulation business with Scientific Software. He discovered high-level mathematics was not his forte, and heard that Sproule was looking for a logging expert for their Panarctic consulting operations. He joined them in 1973, becoming a shareholder in 1975, a Director and manager of engineering in 1980, then vice-president of engineering in 1987. He became president of the company in 1992.

During Glenn's presidency, two new subsidiaries of Sproule Associates Limited were created: Sproule International Limited and Sproule Associates Inc. Both reflect a response to increasing demand for Sproule's services outside Canada. Glenn is credited with encouraging foreign projects like no other president before him.

Glenn has continued to build upon the success of his predecessors and to bring Sproule's name to the forefront of the oil and gas industry. He has been very active in the professional associations to which he belongs, and as a director of the Society of Petroleum Evaluation Engineers' national organization out of Houston (and chairman of the Calgary chapter), he works continuously to ensure the professional integrity of the evaluation industry.

travelled to Calgary for a presentation of the finished document; then several Sproule employees presented the report in Chengdu (the capital of Sichuan Province).

Glenn attributed their success in being awarded the project to doing everything right: "We put the right team of people together, the presidents of each company attended the pre-bid conference, and to make sure the proposal got to the right hands in China, it was delivered in person."

The SPA got its money from the World Bank, and the gas fields are being developed. Sproule has been working in China ever since.

Final Thoughts

In 1969, 75 percent of Sproule's professional employees were geologists and only 25 percent engineers. Today, those numbers are reversed. Despite the geological foundation of the company, Sproule is primarily an evaluation company today, and the majority engineering staff reflects that. Still, geology is the backbone of the evaluation work, and Sproule's geologists have maintained a very active department, undertaking significant geological projects over the last 27 years. That is the legacy of Cam Sproule.

In 1975, Tony Edgington made the following prediction: "We will continue to be one of the most respected and competent consulting firms in the world during the next 25 years, and will be professionally and economically successful." According to Sproule's current president, Glenn Robinson, Tony was "bang on."

Glenn signs the agreement with CNPC. Sitting on his left is Shang Ming Du. Standing, left to right, are Pat Chua (from Sproule), interpreter June Ma, Fangjie Ou, Chang An Liu, and Guiquan Liu. Photo provided by J. Glenn Robinson.

Sproule continues to be one of the leading evaluation companies in Canada, and our success has been the result of our commitment to grow and meet the changing needs of our many clients. I believe our international projects will contribute significantly to the company in the future. This is why Sproule recently created two wholly owned subsidiaries—to handle projects in the United States as well as in other parts of the world. In addition, I anticipate that we will complement our evaluation business by branching into more specialized geological and reservoir engineering services, adding much new talent to our team of experts. In this way, the Sproule group of companies will continue to grow for the next 25 years, and no doubt beyond.

Charlie (left) poses with Stan Harding on their way home from the Hay River area of the Northwest Territories, 1955. Photo provided by Lois Harding.

Charlie Bulmer has been with Sproule almost from the beginning and has set more records in the company than even he was aware of: he was employed by the company for 41 years; he was an Associate for 34 years, a Director for 30 years, and a shareholder for 27 years! He saw the company change its name from J.C. Sproule to J.C. Sproule and Associates Ltd. to Sproule Associates Limited. He saw the oil and gas industry move into the Canadian Arctic, and out again. He saw the heyday of field exploration replaced by a booming evaluation business. Charlie probably knows more about the company than any other employee, past or present.

The company was great for me! Where else would I have had the opportunity to work for a dynamic individual like Cam Sproule and be involved in such a variety of interesting and challenging projects. I have learned much from many people in the company over the years. Cam Sproule hired me and showed faith in me by giving me added responsibilities as I gained knowledge and experience. He was an example to us all in his creativity, determination, work ethic, and goal of perfection in every job done.

Other people who were significant influences in my career include Mickey Crockford, my first mentor; Stan Harding, my party chief in the Northwest Territories; and Tony Edgington and Earl Miller, who taught me much about the financial and business side of the company. The company has been successful because of the dedication to quality of work and professional ethics set originally by professionals such as these. These principles, combined with the energy and drive of the present shareholders and staff, should be the blueprint for many more years of success.

Charlie consults at the Sproule offices, 1997. Photo provided by Sproule Associates.

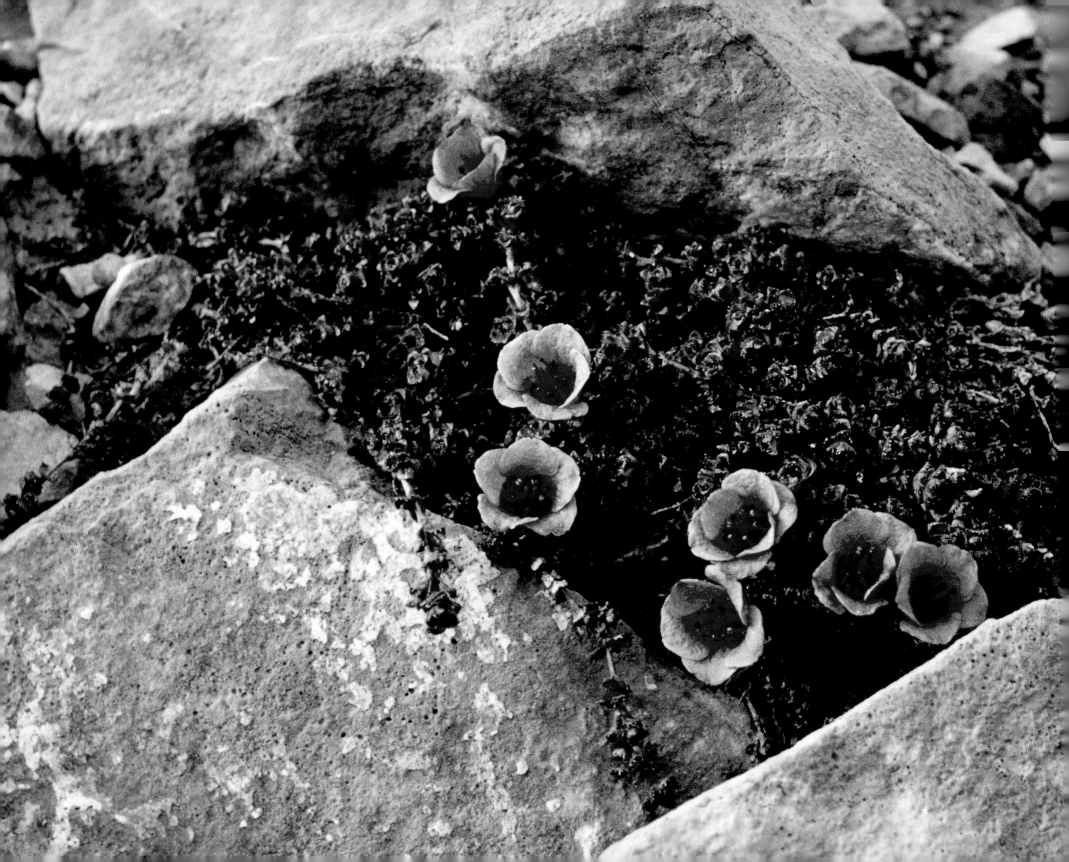

EPILOGUE

    Almost fifty years after a visionary geologist arrived in Calgary and started offering exploration and evaluation services to the oil and gas industry, Sproule has become a world-renowned consulting company. The keys to its success have been the leadership of four presidents and the support of the company's shareholders and all staff members. The company has also been able to adapt in a highly volatile industry. Perhaps most important, they have always worked by the principles of founder John Campbell Sproule—honesty and hard work. Although Cam Sproule's passion was exploration geology, he would be proud to see the tremendous accomplishments on both the geological and the engineering sides of the company. He might not have predicted that the company would make such strides into the international marketplace—enough to warrant formation of two subsidiaries—but he would not have been surprised that Sproule would lead the oil and gas evaluation business into the 21st century.

Purple saxifrage celebrates the short Arctic summer with a blaze of colour. Photo provided by Sproule Associates.

Index